Dear Success Seeker

To Bruce,
The Best is yet to come!
God Bless,
Michele Wright

Dear Success Seeker

Wisdom from Outstanding Women

Michele R. Wright, PhD

ATRIA PAPERBACK
New York   London   Sydney   Toronto

ATRIA PAPERBACK

A Division of Simon & Schuster, Inc.
1230 Avenue of the Americas
New York, NY 10020

First Atria Paperback edition April 2009

ATRIA PAPERBACK and colophon are trademarks of Simon & Schuster, Inc.

For information about special discounts for bulk purchases, please contact Simon & Schuster Special Sales at 1-866-506-1949 or business@simonandschuster.com.

The Simon & Schuster Speakers Bureau can bring authors to your live event. For more information, or to book an event, contact the Simon & Schuster Speakers Bureau at 1-866-248-3049 or visit our website at www.simonspeakers.com.

Designed by Laura Lindgren

Manufactured in the United States of America

10   9   8   7   6   5   4   3   2   1

Library of Congress Cataloging-in-Publication Data

Dear success seeker : career wisdom from outstanding women / [edited by] Michele R. Wright. — 1st Atria paperback ed.
   p. cm.
 Includes bibliographical references and index.
 1. Women—Psychology—Miscellanea. 2. Women—Conduct of life—Miscellanea.
3. Women in public life—Biography. 4. Women in public life—Correspondence.
5. Celebrities—Biography. 6. Celebrities—Correspondence. 7. Vocational guidance. I. Wright, Michele R. (Michele Rhonda) II. Title.

 HQ1206.D358 2009
 650.1082—dc22

                          2008053474
ISBN-13: 978-1-4165-7079-0
ISBN-10:   1-4165-7079-9

DEDICATION

I humbly dedicate *Dear Success Seeker* to the Omnipotent, Omniscient, Omnipresent God, the head of my life, as well as the three most important and influential people in my life: my kind, loving and faithful husband, Terry Gene Wright; and both my supportive, nurturing, and "wise" parents, Frankie Berry Wise and Garland Wise. Mama and Daddy, I was birthed to be Wise and not only in name but in substance. And ultimately that wisdom propelled me to the "right" hand of Mr. Wright! The steadfast belief that each of you had in me from the inception to the completion of this book project has been priceless. I sincerely honor, wholeheartedly love, and greatly respect all three of you for fulfilling your God-given purpose toward my destiny and for my life!

Graciously and Wisely,
Michele Rhonda Wright

ACKNOWLEDGMENTS

- Foremost, to God—the Head of my life—be all the Glory! Thank you, Jesus, for anointing and making the *Dear Success Seeker* project a blessing to all who partake. As your Word states (2 Corinthians 13:11), "Be perfect, be of good comfort, be of one mind, live in peace; and the God of love and peace shall be with you."

- To Terry Gene Wright—my husband, soul mate, best friend, confidant, personal fitness trainer, and the love of my life: Thank you for your countless hours of support in making this project a reality. In this puzzle of life, I thank God for joining us to make a "perfect fit"—and "What therefore God hath joined together, let not man put asunder" (Matthew 19:6). As always, when I count my blessings, I count you twice!!

- To Frankie and Garland Wise—my parents, role models, inspiration, and continuous support base: Thank you for your unconditional love, support, and highest confidence in me as well as in bringing this book to fruition. I am extremely grateful for how you "together" have helped to shape my life. Congratulations on almost 45 years of marriage and best wishes for many more. I'm everything I am because you loved me.

- To Doris Rutledge Parham and Nan Wise—my grandmothers and lifeline: Thank you for helping to shape and make my life. Alongside my parents, you taught me the highest quality of principles and instilled in me how to be "the best of the best."

Your priceless love, unshakable faith, and tireless support for our family will be valued and embraced for many generations to come.

- To Monica René Wise and Marshalette Rolanda Wise—my sisters and pals: Thank you, Monica, for helping to develop my technical/engineering skills and teaching me "who should I admire most"; and thank you, Marshalette, for believing in me and teaching me how to be a big sister. Monica, don't lose your lifelong love and talent for drama/theatre and the performing arts, and Marshalette, don't lose your lifelong passion and vision for the WISE Scholars Foundation.

- To John Atchison—my personal friend and personal project adviser: Thanks for your loving friendship, spiritual guidance, and timely support in helping me to make invaluable connections for this project. You are a great asset to God's ministry, as well as my life.

- To Dr. Camille Cosby—a mentor and role model: Thanks for writing a most heartfelt foreword. Your life and words of wisdom are a constant inspiration to society in general and me in particular. You exemplify success in the rarest form. When I grow up, I want to be just like you.

- To Sondra Pugh, David Brokaw, and Joel Brokaw: Thanks wholeheartedly for assisting me in the effective and efficient flow of crucial information for this project. You were always cheerfully and humbly willing to offer your most valued assistance and high level of expertise.

- To Joan Holman—my dearest friend and book consultant: Thanks for your enormous willingness and energy invested in the vision and fulfillment of *Dear Success Seeker*. Your effort and contributions have been inestimable. You are truly God-sent. I look forward to a lasting comradeship.

- To Gayle King—a woman of excellence and a lady that I admire: I salute you and personally commend you for taking precious time out of your most busy schedule to help bless this project. I thoroughly enjoyed our one-on-one interview. Your success advice will no doubt benefit generations to come. You are genuinely a class act to emulate.

- To Sharon Pinnix Townsend—a great support base and visionary: Thanks so dearly for your confidence, contributions, and support throughout this entire book endeavor. Your positive attitude and professional perspectives were greatly appreciated and valued.

- To Larry Davis—my truest friend and personal photographer: Thanks for a friendship that has lasted an eternity. You have always been an integral part of my life, helping to seize my most special moments with your most special portraits.

- To Vaniece Sinawski—my beautiful friend and beauty consultant: Thanks for always being there to make me feel beautiful both inside and out. Your friendship is a rarity. You are a friend among friends.

- To Ronald Scott McDowell—my lifelong buddy and personal artist: Thanks for your unique depictions of the various stages of my life. You have captured not only my soul on canvas, but also my heart as an everlasting friend.

- To Barbara Danner—my supporter and counselor: Thanks for being a true trailblazer and believing in this undertaking. Your perspectives and advice throughout this entire project have been invaluable. I look forward to working in synergy with you on numerous future projects.

- To Pastor Lonnie Aaron and First Lady Mary Aaron—my former Pastor and First Lady: Thanks for your Godly spiritual guidance and the planted seeds of hope, faith, and love (*the greatest of these is love*). You both truly helped to lay the groundwork of the precious name of Jesus in my life—for Jesus Christ is God, Lord of All, King of Kings.

- To Pastor Lloyd Lasker Jr. and First Lady Stella Lasker—my current Pastor and First Lady: I thank God for your friendship, spiritual guidance, and most anointed knowledge, wisdom, and understanding. Thank you for teaching me not only that Jesus is God, but "God is love; and he that dwelleth in love dwelleth in God, and God in him" (1 John 4:16).

· To Yasma Stringer and Stacie Vanover—two of my closest friends and confidantes: Thank you both for your tireless efforts and advice concerning the final stages of this book endeavor. Your heartfelt love, encouragement, and advice were unparalleled. You both truly exemplify the realness and miracle of friendship.

· To Rita Rosenkranz and Krishan Trotman—my literary agent and publishing editor: Thank you so much for stepping out on faith and seeing the merits, uniqueness, and vision of this book project. You both strongly believed and supported not only this endeavor but me personally as an author. Your levels of professionalism and expertise are the best, bar none. You are truly an invaluable duo with whom I look forward to forging a lifelong affiliation.

· To Amy Tannenbaum—my newly acquired publishing editor: Thank you for graciously, cheerfully, and proudly assuming responsibility for the timely and successful completion of *Dear Success Seeker*. Working with you has been a most joyous and rewarding experience. I look forward to teaming with you on future book endeavors.

· And last but not least—Thanks to all the women who contributed to *Dear Success Seeker* and for touching the lives of all the countless "success seekers" who will benefit from your words of wisdom. You truly exemplify a spirit of excellence!

Wholeheartedly,
Michele Rhonda Wright

Dear Success Seeker

Introduction

MICHELE R. WRIGHT, PhD

It is a pleasure to introduce *Dear Success Seeker*, a book that has fashioned "success letters" from eighty-three outstanding women achievers and features an eloquent foreword by author, educator, philanthropist, and producer Camille O. Cosby; alongside an exclusive personal interview with Gayle King, editor-at-large of *O, The Oprah Magazine*. These notable contributors, who represent a unique, diverse, and multicultural group of both famed and unsung achievers, have both individually and collectively created a synergistic success roadmap for success seekers from all walks of life.

When I reflect over my roadblocks to success, including an extensive learning disability, a severe speech impediment resulting in my inability to speak before the age of five, and an extremely short attention span, I am quickly and humbly reminded of how essential it is to have champions of success in our lives to help inspire us toward our own successes of life. I was very fortunate to have loving and wise parents who did not accept my perceived shortcomings as an excuse for failure, and to have a devoted and God-fearing husband who graciously championed and supported my numerous success endeavors. Needless to say, they empowered me to fervently strive to achieve my full success potential.

With this support, I journeyed ahead to receive a Bachelor of Science degree in electrical engineering, graduating with High Honors and as "Electrical Engineering Student of the Year" from Tuskegee University; became the first African-American to receive a Master of Science in Engineering Management and Industrial Engineering from the University of Tennessee Space Institute; and received my Doctor of Philosophy in Public Policy from the University of Arkansas at Fayetteville. Additionally, I have had a twenty-plus-year career as a top-performing and award-winning corporate professional.

Bottom line: if success was achievable by me, then it is conceivable by you. However, it is important to have success warriors who can assist in your personal and professional success journey. The contributors of *Dear Success Seeker* provide great inspiration and invaluable advice to success seekers from a wide variety of backgrounds and talents who are striving to achieve optimal career and life success. Each letter begins with "Dear Success Seeker" to personally address the diverse individuality of our readers.

The women in this book represent a wealth of life-experiences and a multitude of talents. As Gayle King profoundly states, "Be prepared when opportunity presents itself." I am confident that the words of wisdom and passionate spirit that the outstanding women achievers in *Dear Success Seeker* have shared will not only prepare readers to maximize their opportunities, but also undoubtedly equip them for achieving success in all aspects of life.

Enjoy this book and savor every priceless word of wisdom; then certainly you will be equipped with the necessary tools to be successful, and one day go out to invest in the lives of others.

Love and God Bless,
Michele Rhonda Wright

Contributors

Camille O. Cosby, Foreword 9
Gayle King, Exclusive Interview 11

Book Participants

Foreword

CAMILLE O. COSBY, EdD

Author, *A Wealth of Wisdom*

Michele R. Wright has so astutely asked successful women who represent myriad ethnicities, ages, and careers to speak for themselves and tell us about their wisdom and experiences.

Most women are acutely aware of the responsibilities that come with success. That sense of responsibility is ingrained in us as women. But do we act on our awareness?

Success has different meanings to different people. *Merriam-Webster's Unabridged Dictionary* defines success as "the degree or measure of attaining a desired end." So, what have been the measures of attainment for my success?

Simply put, three words: *family, integrity,* and *"doing."* The family is the foundation upon which all our success is built. We cannot succeed alone. I have seen numerous people put their work ahead of family or loved ones and eventually pay a tremendous price. Resentment and alienation will be the cost to pay. Clearly, we cannot take our loved ones for granted. We must communicate, nurture, and be visibly loving. Otherwise, how can we receive love in return? Many of us can relate to the impositions that give us less time with our families, whether job related or due to other things that take up our time and attention. But aren't we just using these setbacks as excuses to deny ourselves emotional intimacy with our families or loved ones? The fear of emotional intimacy is a success bankruptcy. We must cultivate deep relationships to achieve good success.

Let us revive the word *integrity* and act out its true meaning. Do we succeed at the expense of others? Do we lie or cheat to get ahead? Or do we share our knowledge, function as helpers, and do what we can so that others can benefit as well as ourselves? Success is always more meaningful when we are respectful of others' and nature's myriad beauties.

As my father often said, "The proof is in the pudding." Don't just talk it, do it. The doing is definitely the proof. Humans seem to be more willing to do if they have passion about what they do. Some might say, "That's easy for Camille Cosby to say." Yes, it is. For example, I have never believed that anyone should compromise his or her talents or goals to earn fast money. Even if it is a job offer that is difficult to refuse—a higher salary, better opportunities, etc.—if it is not what you love to do! Too often, I've noticed that people are less productive in life because they are not happy with what they're doing. Joyful attitudes and behaviors make for excellent mental and physical health.

Frequently, we attract what we exude. If we show love to our families or loved ones, we will likely have dedicated and respectful people around us; if we have integrity, we will be treated with integrity; and if we are doers, that energy will be felt and willingly imitated by others to do for us.

—Camille O. Cosby

Exclusive Interview

Gayle King
(Editor-at-Large, *O, The Oprah Magazine*)

and Michele R. Wright

Michele: How do you personally define success?

Gayle: Success means so many different things to different people. As you progress in life, even your own definition of success changes. Throughout my life, success has been about my career, having children, and having a good marriage. Things don't always work out the way you plan, so your definition changes. Every woman has to determine her own definition because what may be successful for you may not be successful for me. Success is very personal.

Michele: Congratulations on your great success as editor-at-large of *O, The Oprah Magazine* and as host of *The Gayle King Show* on the Oprah & Friends XM channel. *O* was the most successful magazine launch in history. What factors contributed to that success?

Gayle: I am very proud of *O Magazine.* The factors that made it such a success are Oprah, Oprah, and Oprah! If you look at the magazine, it clearly has Oprah's hand in it in every step of the way. But I also know that if people didn't like the magazine, it wouldn't matter how beloved she was. But no one underestimates the advantage that Oprah gives. We really talk about Oprah's philosophy of "you are your own best self," and we want women to see that. You'll never see in our magazine thirty tips in thirty days for thin thighs, because we want women to accept what they have. We have a great line around here: "looking for happiness in all the right places," and it always starts with you.

Michele: During your years in television, you have won three Emmy Awards. Would you expound on how you achieved this magnitude of success?

Gayle: People always say that when they watch me on TV, they really feel they know me; and that is one of the highest compliments you can give me. I really don't know how to do or be anything else. If you make mistakes, that's okay, you keep right on going. I have an ability to be myself on television. And by that I mean flaws and all.

Michele: Did you always know what you wanted your career path to be?

Gayle: I have always enjoyed talking to people, from the time I was a little kid. I am a really big people person, so I knew I had to do something that would allow me to interact with people. I did not know it was going to be television or anything in the media, because I was told at a very early age by my grandmother that Mother Nature hadn't been as kind to me as she'd been to other little girls. But I started interning at a TV station and became hooked on the business of TV.

And I marvel as I sit here today working at one of the top magazines in the country, because I didn't have any magazine experience. And Oprah came to me and talked about this job and I initially said, "I'm not interested in magazines; I don't know anything about magazines." And she said, "Yeah, but you know a good story and you know me." They needed someone in New York who had Oprah's sensibility and an understanding of what she would want in a magazine. So I'm here, and I know that I make a difference. I am honored to be here and be a part of the Oprah brand.

Michele: What would you say to women who have no idea what they want to do in terms of a career?

Gayle: I remember going to college at the University of Maryland, sitting there at registration and having to declare my major. As a freshman, I had no clue. I was sitting there with the registration book trying to figure out what could I be, what should I do, what should I take. I knew I was never good at math and sciences. But I've been very good in reading and writing since I was a kid. I lived in Turkey as a child, and we didn't have TV, so we always had to do a lot of reading. And I looked at the course selection thinking what could I do that has a lot of reading and writing. "Psychology." So I majored in psychology, intending to go into child psychology, or go to law school.

And then I got a job at a TV station my sophomore/junior year in college. I was working at a camera store and one of the mucky-mucks at the station [Channel 9 in Washington] started talking to me because I was always friendly and very helpful. He asked if I'd ever thought about TV, because I had a very nice speaking voice. I replied, "No, I've never thought about that." He said, "Well, we have an entry-level job in the newsroom; would you be interested?" My question to him was, "Do I have to work weekends?"—because I was already working two other jobs. He said, "No." So I went and tried it and I was just hooked. I kind of fell into it. It's like opportunity presented itself to me. So, to me, you have to be open to things, but please don't ever ignore something that you feel passionate about.

I continually work with my children in hope that they find something they love to do. I think the best thing you can do is find something that you love to do and get paid for it—a job that you would want to do even if they didn't pay you a cent.

Michele: What place do you think spirituality has in the workplace? There is a lot of talk about that now.

Gayle: Spirituality helps center you and helps make you a better person. I don't think it should just be restricted to the workplace. It should be a way that you live your life. I don't know how people who have no spiritual grounding succeed in anything—in personal or professional relationships. Spirituality sort of centers you, I believe. I just feel that spirituality is a way of living your life and striving to be the best that you can be—it's kindness and consideration of others, whether it's personal or professional.

Michele: Do you see more opportunities for career success for women?

Gayle: We certainly have more options today, and I think we are taking advantage of those options. The beauty of this world today is that you have the options to decide exactly what you want to do, what works best for you. And I like that.

Michele: How do you think women can change the world for the better? What are the issues facing the women of today?

Gayle: Stay focused on what works for you. So many people spend their lives trying to work out somebody else's plan, instead of figuring out what works best for them. Stick with your plan, instead of looking at what she's doing over there because her life seems to be great.

You never know what is going on in somebody else's life. You have to figure out what works best for you and stick with that plan. And you're the only one who knows the answer to that question. You can't get it from your mom; you can't get it from your friends. You're the only one who knows in your heart of hearts what works best for you.

Michele: What advice would you give to women about developing their careers?

Gayle: Find a career that you really enjoy and then find someone who's doing that. Then figure out a way to either make contact with them or get contact in that field. Nothing beats the personal experience of working—whether it's television, whether it's magazines, whether it's cooking. What I find very interesting is that successful people really don't mind helping others who they believe have some initiative. There are some who are going to be jerks and not interested in sharing, but most people are very flattered when you ask them. So, once you decide what [your field] is, it's good to try different things. Don't be afraid to start at the bottom and work your way up. You will learn a lot of things down there, a lot of things that will be very helpful to you later in life.

Michele: Throughout your many life experiences, what were your proudest moments? And I won't say "proudest" moment because I'm sure there are several.

Gayle: I think that I have touched some people along the way.

Somebody called me out of the blue the other day and said she was pregnant and wanted me to adopt her child—because she's seen me, she's seen interviews with me, and she sees how I talk about my children—and she didn't think she could give that to her children. I thought that was very flattering, but I know that's not something I could do. So I'm proud that people at least perceive me as a very kind human being.

And I still feel that I'm always learning and always growing. Even now as I sit here at this age, I'm still thinking: what can I do to be better? You can always learn, and as long as you're doing something that you love, you don't feel old. Because old isn't what I feel. I still feel like such a kid. So there's something very exciting about that.

Michele: In every success there are trials and tribulations. What were your greatest obstacles and how did you deal with them?

Gayle: I had a talk show that was canceled. On another occasion, I got called into the office after I had my second baby and was told that my butt was too big. You know things you think: "I can't believe he just said that to me." Those are learning experiences. I take any kind of adversity and try to use it as a learning experience—what am I supposed to learn from this? Throughout any type of pain, we learn and grow.

I am also a firm believer that everything happens for a reason. So, while it was very upsetting when my show was canceled, my kids were so sweet to me during that time. And I was saying to them that when you have a setback, you have to get up and you have to keep going. Of course it hurts, and you feel it, but you can't allow that to take away your confidence or make you feel less about yourself. Oprah has a great line that failure is just God's way of saying let's move in another direction. Let's try something else. So rather than sitting and wallowing in it, think, "Well, maybe I do need to try something else." I believe when one door closes, another one opens. So you just try something else.

Michele: Gayle, like you, I love to start my day with a good breakfast—especially with one of your favorites, Art's lemon pancakes. What other things do you like to do to ensure the start of a successful day?

Gayle: You have to be a confident person even if you don't feel so confident. Starting a day successfully is a matter of being informed with whatever your business is. Whatever it is, *know your business.* You can't go to business without being prepared. I don't want my children to ever think mediocrity is okay. So, from the time they were very young, I always said, "Please, please, please always do more than what the teacher asked. Don't go through life just skating by and doing things at the last minute." Start your day with good habits.

Mary Aaron

First Lady,
Bibleway Community Church

Dear Success Seeker . . .

Success is like a traveler setting out to reach a particular destination. She starts out traveling the maximum speed limit. But the road is not straight. She has to reduce her speed for curves, loops, speed bumps, construction sites, caution lights, and maybe a brief delay due to a flat tire. These might slow her down, but with the determination to reach her destination, she does not dare give up. She must keep traveling. The saying is true, "a quitter doesn't win, and a winner doesn't quit."

Success comes in cans. "I can, you can, we all can," especially when we put trust in one God. My personal experience comes from stamina, loving people, respecting others, willingness. These traits were put in me as a child.

Life has many struggles, and in the midst of your struggles, the goal may seem unreachable; but you'll be fine if you pop the trunk of your intuition, put on that spare tire of strong determination, and make sure that you check the oil of perseverance in your engine. Put your complete trust in God to do the driving, and you will surely be successful.

Sincerely,
Mary Aaron

Valerie B. Ackerman

President of USA Basketball;
Former President of WNBA

Dear Success Seeker . . .

I believe the keys to having a successful and happy life are: don't be afraid to try new things and take chances; try to find a line of work that you're passionate about, because when you're enthusiastic about what you do, you'll probably excel at it; and be sure to have balance in your life: make time for family, friends, vacations, exercise, and personal activities, and "recharge your batteries" on a regular basis. Remember that relationships are important. If you treat other people with kindness and respect, they'll more likely treat you that way in return. Never forget that life is a journey, and the best part of the experience is in the ride itself, not the destination. So enjoy it!

Best of luck,
Valerie B. Ackerman

Vernell G. Anderson

Former Director of EEO Programs with the Federal Government

Dear Success Seeker . . .

The measure of success is often determined by the goals one sets for oneself. One of the things you will learn is that there is no simple way to define or achieve success. Success is as varied as the people who achieve it. Likewise, to some extent what constitutes success has to be determined by the individual. My personal belief is based on Matthew 6:33, which instructs us to seek God and his righteousness first and all other things will be added. Society has in place some general standards that measure success, but in reality it does not go far enough. Many people achieve great success and never receive formal recognition. Therefore, one's success has to be determined by one's determination to achieve a specific goal.

Determine what you want to accomplish in life. You must set attainable goals that will allow you to achieve the results you desire.

There are some very critical and necessary attributes you will need to possess as you pursue your desired goal(s). The ones I have listed are certainly not all-inclusive, and you are likely to add others as you develop and achieve your own level of success. These are the ones that I have found useful in practically every situation.

- *Having a positive attitude:* It has been said that attitude determines altitude. A positive attitude will help you view issues and see opportunities that others often miss. It will also open doors that will be closed to those with negative attitudes. You will also want to surround yourself with like-minded positive people.
- *Staying focused:* Once you have determined what your goal is, keep it before you. Outline or plan specific steps that you will need to take. Following your outline or plan will help you to stay focused.
- *Working hard:* Being willing to work hard is critical to your achieving your desired level of success. Hard work is one of the cornerstones of success. Not only will it help you to achieve success it will help you appreciate your accomplishments once you achieve them.
- *Being persistent with determination:* This is the willingness to give it another try. Persistence is getting up one more time after you're knocked down. Persistence and determination mean you will find a way, while others find excuses.

In the words of Proverbs 23:12, "apply your heart to instruction, and your ears to words of knowledge," and you will have found the secret to spiritual, professional, and personal success.

Your success will be determined by you, and you can make a difference not just for yourself but for the world.

As you plan your future, my very best wishes and God's richest blessings be with you.

Sincerely,
Vernell G. Anderson

Edith Virginiabell Atchison

Mother

Dear Success Seeker . . .

As a child growing up, my parents taught me the importance of being nice. They would encourage me to look for the good in people; not to be judgmental or negatively critical of others. Saying things that would hurt someone's feelings was not the Christian thing to do. People who impressed me and had an influence in my life was anyone who was nice. I believe the Bible is the one book we all should read. When I was growing up as a child, I thought everyone did. There were two things I taught my children, read your Bible and be nice to people.

God's continued blessing,
Edith V. Atchison

Regina M. Benjamin, MD

First African-American Woman elected to the American Medical Association Board of Trustees

Dear Success Seeker . . .

Success is a journey, a trip to enjoy along the way. It is a verb, not a noun. It is something you do, not something you are.

It has been said that you make a living by what you get, but you make a life by what you give. It is certainly important to make a good living and provide for you and your families' needs, but it is just as important to help others.

Establishing my Rural Health Clinic to provide quality health care to those who otherwise may not receive it has brought more joy to my life than any paycheck ever could. The look on a mother's face when I tell her that her baby is going to be okay is priceless. Whether her baby is age four or forty-four, the look on her face is the same.

Whatever your passion, you can always find a way to put it to use to help someone else. So I encourage you to be good at what you do, and then do Good!

Sincerely,
Regina M. Benjamin

Margaret Louise Betts, MD

President, Betts Medical Group

Dear Success Seeker . . .

Aunt Sally, "Auntie," prayed daily that one of Mauge's chillen would 'mount to some'm.

Daddy's undying love for all five of his children made all of the trials and tribulations of a little fat girl in a poor dysfunctional family seem like a big platform meant to be rearranged and turned right side up! Yes, this little black girl, who moved ten times before finishing the sixth grade, a special-education student, was very special and I knew it!

Sally Shields Brown was the oldest of my mother's siblings. My mother, Margaret Shields Betts, was the youngest. She left home at the age of eleven and had her first child by age thirteen. Some four husbands and eleven pregnancies later, I, Margaret Louise Betts, was born. My parents split up after numerous confrontations between my father and my older brother due to my mother's inability to choose the right side. One altercation left my father on crutches with a broken leg.

After he left, I longed for his presence, his strength, his power, and his love. He, too, like a magnet needed and wanted to be with his children. Some of our family moving was a direct attempt by my mother to hide us from my father. But, like a tiger without its cubs and all of those animal instincts, my father, Willie Edward Betts, managed to find us each time.

I remember one Christmas when he wanted to have the four of us with him all night. At that time he boarded a room with a family because that was all he could afford. All I can remember in the room was a big bed, a chair, and a Christmas tree. We, my two older sisters and one younger brother, slept in his bed as he slept the entire night in the chair, with his eye fixed on us! . . . Love . . . Power . . . Strength . . . and Commitment!

My father remarried a lady, Mary Mays, who turned out to be my guardian angel. A lady who truly loved the Lord and us and displayed this with her words, deeds, and prayers of cause. Sometime after this I asked my mother, "Can I live with my daddy?" and she said, "Yes!" Looking back, I recall that I was the fifth child that my mother gave away!

My move to my father and stepmother's house helped me realize how successful I could be!

I was fortunate that I now had a loving environment, caring parents who loved, prayed for, guided, and protected me. They helped me realize what my life could be if only I stayed focused. My father, a tall, dark, determined man with a third-grade education, was oh so wise. He repeated over and over again, "It's not no until you say it's no!" I gradually learned how to say Yes! Yes! Yes!

I had made my professional aspiration known to anyone who would listen by the time I was eleven or twelve. My mother used to say "you got it honest!" over and over again. By the time I finally asked her what she meant, some ten to fifteen years later, I had already graduated from medical school. She told me the story of my birth, which had a profound effect on me, and I was forever changed and reassured.

When I was born, labor and delivery took place mostly in the home, and I was named after two midwives. One was my great-grandmother, Margaret. Great-grandmother Margaret was a very dark, large-boned woman with long white braids who rode side-saddle on a white horse from town to town caring for those in need of medical attention. So you see, my great-grandmother lives today in me through my profession as a medical doctor. You must connect with your past so that you will know if *"you got it honest."* Sit with and talk with your elders. They will help you realize your worth and responsibility to yourself, your God, and society.

These are my accomplishments . . . so far!

- Born to Margaret Shield Betts
- The proud daughter of Willie Edward Betts Sr.
- Blessed to be raised by Mary Mays Betts
- A special-education student in the first grade
- A teenage mother at age fifteen
- A high school graduate at age seventeen
- A certified radiology technologist
- A doctorate degree from the Medical College of Ohio—in private practice for twenty-one years
- Married the only male my father approved of, now divorced
- The dedicated mother of three "adults"
- An elected public official—the Detroit Board of Education—three times
- Owner of a local magazine, publication suspended
- A community activist with Board appointments
- A Child of the King, Trustee and Chair of Youth Council in my church
- CEO, the Betts Foundation

Good luck to you in all of your endeavors, and remember: It's not no until you say it's no!

Margaret Louise Betts

Pastor Shirley Caesar

Grammy Award—winning Gospel Musician

Dear Success Seeker . . .

It is my premise that from the first day a child enters grade school, every minute should count. Education and time in school must be taken very seriously.

You are the future . . . which means you are our future doctors, lawyers, pastors, parents, school teachers, engineers, Supreme Court justices, and presidents. It is my opinion that each day there should be a special time set aside just for study . . . allowing nothing, if possible, to interfere with study time.

Success begins in your mind and in your heart. Your attitude must be positive and your heart contrite. You must be proactive and forthright in your actions. Seek God's plan and purpose for your life and then remain steadfast in your pursuits.

As I always say, Jesus plus education equals success!

With love,
Shirley Caesar

Mildred H. Carter

**First Licensed Female Aviator in
the Civilian Pilot Training Program,
the school that became legendary with the success
of the Tuskegee Airmen in World War II**

Dear Success Seeker . . .

What can I tell you about my life experiences that will be helpful to you as you journey into the future? I can tell you to be brave, have confidence in your God-given talents and abilities, and go for it!

Let me relate to you the story of a girl, a young student at Tuskegee Institute back in the early 1940s before America entered World War II. I was working as a work student on the campus in the office where young men were coming in by the dozens to apply for a program called the Civilian Pilot Training Program (CPTP). They were going to learn to fly airplanes! What an opportunity for them, and why not for me? I applied also and was told that I was two weeks too young. You had to be eighteen by September 1, and my eighteenth birthday was September 14. So, I had to sit back and watch the young men finish the primary flight training and go into the secondary flight training before I could resubmit my application. But remember, young people, persistence does pay off. I applied again and this time was accepted. If I could pass the flight physical, complete the ground-school classes at night, while doing my flight training work, I would be on my way. However, I was a senior in the School of Business at this time, so one would wonder who could find the time to do all of this. Again, persistence pays off. I began flight training, successfully soloed after about eight hours of dual instruction, and was on my way to earning the private pilots' license. Oh happy day! On February 1, 1941, I was certified by the Federal Aviation Agency (FAA) as a licensed private pilot!

Follow your dreams.

Sincerely,
Mildred H. Carter

Chérie Carter-Scott, PhD

New York Times Bestselling International Author

Dear Success Seeker . . .

We live in exciting and confusing times. There is more opportunity for young women to make their lives everything they dreamed than ever before in history. There is also more competition than ever before. We have more capabilities in technology, communication, and transportation than ever before, and there are people suffering, starving, and at war. So many opposite realities can create confusion, so it's important for you to know where to turn for direction, advice, and support.

If the world judges you as successful, it means that you have either realized your own goals and expectations or you may have exceeded normal, average standards held by the majority of people. Accomplishments are the main barometer the world uses to measure success: breaking records, amassing fortunes, being the first to do something, or changing mind-sets of current realities all qualify.

Being the best at something, conquering, curing, breaking though some barriers, all deem one eligible to enter the hallowed halls of success. Ask yourself: what is the difference between success and fulfillment? I discovered that success is measured primarily by standards outside ourselves, while fulfillment is assessed internally. No one can deem you fulfilled except you. However, the world, with its objective criteria, can and does judge you as successful if you measure up to its standards. When your own sense of well-being and the external symbols of accomplishment converge, then you have achieved "success."

I wish for you the discovery of your inner truths, the conviction to believe in yourself, the wherewithal to find your way, and the courage to rise when the world expects you to fall. May you learn the lessons life places before you and accomplish all that will provide you with deep, authentic fulfillment and happiness.

Enjoy the journey.

Blessings,
Chérie Carter-Scott

Vanessa Castagna

**One of *Fortune* Magazine's "50 Most Powerful Women
in Business"; Former Chairwoman of Mervyn's
Department Stores and JCPenney Stores,
Catalog and Internet**

Dear Success Seeker . . .

From the time I was a child, I always took it for granted that
women could succeed. I come from a family that has had three
generations of women who pursued active careers.

I've learned from champions in all walks of life. They've taught
me to *never, never accept the status quo*—to constantly focus on improving
my abilities to perform at a higher level.

One champion in particular is Jack Welch, former CEO of
General Electric. Jack is a legendary maverick—the gold standard
against which other CEOs are measured. I would recommend you
read his book *Jack Welch & The G.E. Way.* His defining credo is: "By
reaching for the seemingly impossible, you often do the impossible."

Open your hearts and minds to those champions who can
make a positive impact on your life. Never stop learning! We live

in a world that is constantly changing. My challenge to you is to become a leader of change. Energize the people around you.

Every one of us can be successful. Our possibilities are as limitless as our imaginations. Stretch yourself—*reach for your dreams!*

Sincerely,
Vanessa Castagna

Leeann Chin

Founder of Leeann Chin, Inc., a $40 million Chinese-American Fast Food Restaurant Chain

Dear Success Seeker . . .

When I was growing up in China, a good future for a woman came almost entirely from marrying a wealthy husband and keeping a good home. Very little opportunity presented itself. Young women in China were not supposed to work and, in fact, were told to not come across as too smart, for fear no man would want them. Most girls didn't attend high school. However, I never sought my good future by marrying a rich man and I studied hard. I wanted to do more with my life, to create something, to make something of myself, to do work that could help other people. I learned this about myself when I was about thirteen. World War II had just ended and no one could leave their homes. We stayed at home for a very long time, only rarely getting out. I began to knit. I learned everything I could about knitting. Soon I began teaching others how to knit. My relatives became nervous. "Why do you teach everyone your knowledge?" "Keep it to yourself?" I explained to them that when I teach, I learn. My passion for knitting led me to make many items of clothing using intricate and complex stitches.

The more I taught others, the more I learned. I found myself most satisfied when others learned from me. I never looked for what I might get in return. I just felt lucky that people wanted to learn from me.

My siblings and I would show our parents our report cards. Even when we had good report cards they would not praise us. We could only hope to hear them say "good job," but always we were asked to consider what more we could do. This is how I grew up. My father ran a store. When I was sixteen, the Communists came into power and we could no longer keep our employees. I began to help my father by counting money. I used my abacus. I was quick at counting. One day I overheard some people commenting to my parents how smart I must be to count so well at my age. After the people left, my mother reminded me in passing, "Don't be so happy, the people are just being nice to us. You are not that special." That day I looked for a way to improve my counting. Today I have immense opportunity in something I can do well that has become my passion, the food business. Because of this, I give as much of myself as I can. You will find that you can give a lot of yourself, and the more you give, the more you get in return.

With every report card, every improvement in my counting, and today, every day in the food business, I know never to be too sure of myself. You can never learn too much, know too much. Always improve yourself. When I first began in business, I was not so sure of my capabilities. All I knew was that I must work extremely hard. When believing in yourself becomes difficult, then believe that you can keep working and work harder. With that attitude, believing in yourself will come. Often it comes after you have found a way to make something better, a way to improve. When my father would commend me on my grades, "Don't be too happy with yourself. Can you do better?" he was channeling my energy into finding ways I might improve so I wouldn't waste it on satisfaction.

When I began my food business, I sought to learn everything I could about food and cooking. Teaching others my recipes and my way of cooking and watching them create something wonderful has become the most enjoyable part of my work.

You have many opportunities in front of you. I encourage you to find something that you can do well and have passion for. Working is incredibly important, but when you work passionately at something, you will work with energy and you will have good future.

Growing up in China, we all knew America could provide immense opportunity for those willing to work really hard. I found this especially true when I started my own business. Nothing has come easy. My rewards have come not from financial success but from having the opportunity to work passionately at something that I can do well.

Many young people tell me they want to make lots of money but I rarely hear young people today share with me their passion. Have passion for your work and labor intensely at it. You will find this a requirement for having a good future.

So, remember, regardless of who you are or where you are from, find something you can do well and have passion for it. You will work for hours and hours on your passion and you will never burn out. This is most certainly true. People won't understand you but they will watch you work, they will notice how dedicated you are, and they will see you having fun. It's pretty amazing when this happens. It has happened to me. Today, I can cook all day and enjoy every minute of it. I love to cook.

Happy cooking,
Leeann Chin

P.S. Never be afraid to apologize or to lose an argument. Arguments are rarely worth it. Apologizing is the first thing you must do when you've made a mistake; sometimes, even when you've done nothing wrong. Just apologize. It's okay. Give people what they want. You'll be a better person for it because once you apologize, you can ask about your mistake. You will hear everything you need to know about how you can improve.

Johnnetta B. Cole, PhD

President Emerita of Bennett College
for Women and Spelman College

Dear Success Seeker . . .

Please, don't ever grow up! You should be a student for the rest of your life. Let me tell you why. A full rich life, a rich life, a complete life, requires lifelong learning. It also requires some of those attributes that are so closely associated with being young: inquisitiveness, enthusiasm, and idealism. Once you turn off your ability to inquire, to imagine, to hypothesize, to think, to learn—you have shut down the most vital part of who you are and who you can become.

Please, do not end up being able to take care of yourself—I mean only yourself. Of course I hope you will become self-sufficient. And so do your parents! But as you dream about your future, I trust those dreams are about more than a closet full of fine clothes and a garage with a fancy car or two. I hope you also dream of the joy of spending Saturday afternoons at a community center tutoring little girls and boys, or helping out in a homeless shelter, or bringing comfort to women in a rape-crisis center.

Remember, doing for others is just the rent you must pay for living on this earth. Continue to look at yourself in a mirror but see many more folks than yourself. As you look at your reflection in a mirror, of course I hope that you will feel good about who you see there, that you will feel self-confident about your own abilities, and I trust you will have respect for all of the folks who look and are like you.

However, our nation will never reach its full potential until we learn to draw on the range of voices, perspectives, and talents of all of our people. We will know our full strength only when we require and use the contributions of people of different religious beliefs, different ages, different sexual orientations, different classes, and, yes, people who are differently able.

In the words of a Chinese saying: one flower never makes a spring.

With every good wish, I am,

Sincerely yours,
Johnnetta Betsch Cole

The Reverend Johnnie Colemon

Founder of Christ Universal Temple, a New Thought Church with Twenty Thousand Members

Dear Success Seeker . . .

You are endowed with unlimited possibilities for good because you have been made in the image-likeness of God and Nothing is impossible for God.

How do I know this? Because I have proven it in my life. In the forty-five years of my ministry, I have established and maintained a thriving church with over thirty-five hundred people in attendance each Sunday; a religious-educational institute; an association of twenty-two churches and study groups located across the USA and abroad; an elementary school; and a banquet facility.

How has this been done? First of all, we must remember that success is not a destination but a journey—a journey that begins with a dream. Whatever your dream may be, please know that it has been placed in your heart and it *is* attainable.

May I offer a few steps that may help as you begin your journey.

1. *Decide* that nothing or no one will dissuade you from accomplishing your dream.

2. *Love* your dream. It must become your passion. Love what you do no matter how insignificant it may seem, for everything that comes into your life is a signpost pointing the way.

3. Have *faith* that what you desire to achieve is needed, that it will be of benefit, not just to you but to humankind. Have faith and then all that is needed will be provided.

4. You must not be afraid to *work*. How do you spell success? W-O-R-K.

5. Think *positive* thoughts about yourself, your dream, about others. No matter what seems to appear, see the good in it; for every experience—good, bad, or indifferent—is an opportunity for growth. Think about what you want, not what you don't want. Thoughts are things. You are the thinker that thinks the thoughts that make the things.

6. *Dispose of* anything in your life that does not support your dream.

7. *Trust God.* "Let go and let God" does not mean you do nothing. Remember, you must work; but know that the inspiration, the guidance you need, is available to you and God will direct your ways.

I salute you as you move toward your goal. Persevere—keep working no matter the seeming challenge.

Be patient—with yourself and with others.

Be bold—dare to go where none have gone before.

Be firm—stand steadfast.

Be determined—you are a powerhouse and you can achieve your dream.

Be blessed!

In His service,
Johnnie Colemon

Marva N. Collins

Founder, Marva Collins Preparatory School

Dear Success Seeker . . .

The word *outstanding* to me means to stand outside the crowd, not to become a member of the popular herd, to listen to the drummer that I hear from within, not to work to keep step with the rest of my fellow men; to be all that God created me to be. The hardest thing on earth for me is to be me. This means that my every waking moment is spent developing and evolving the best me that I can be. I have never betrayed my own mind. I do not live for the opinion of others. I live to make daily deposits to evolve into the best person that I can be. This means making daily and hourly deposits to my "self bank account." I am often terrified that if I do not make the right deposits, my inner self, my *me,* my "self" will end up overdrawn with insufficient deposits.

Our character is the premise of who we decide to be, and not to live on the opinions of others. If I have the subject, and a friend has the verb, we can never write a private sentence. To be self-motivated, self-generated, and self-propelled means that I do not garner a "self" from those around me. My aim in life is to be the very best in whatever I am involved in. I am the best . . . I deserve the best . . . I will work toward achieving the best . . . it is my birthright. These are the first tenets I teach students. All the academics in the world will do us little good if we do not know where we are going, how to get there, and have the ability to see, and the will in pleasure and in pain to travel the roads needed to reach our destination. There, to me, are no failures in life. Failure, to me, is simply a place to rest while we plan the real and true path to success.

How we use time is essential. Time is the raw material of everything. One moment wasted will never be regained. Procrastinating, waiting to do in the future what we could do today, is also a stumbling block to success. Yesterday is history, tomorrow is a mystery . . . right now, this moment is a gift, and that is why it is called The Present. It is a gift, it is a present. Use it wisely, or it returns no more. Each minute can be wasted, abused, but eternity is in each minute.

Life is not always fair to the achiever, but achieve anyway. The greatest ideas can be shot down by the smallest and most cynical minds, but develop great ideas anyway. All the tasks I have ever accomplished that required great determination were those that my friends, foes, and critics declared impossible. Now when I am told something is "impossible," I realize that this is exactly the right choice for me to pursue.

Life is growth; not to move forward is to fall backward. Life remains life so long as it advances. Every step upward opens to man a wider range of action and achievement. There is no final, permanent plateau. Show me the person who has arrived in the Land of the Done and I will show you someone who has ceased being outstanding. We are always in the stress of knowing that average people are never in short supply. One can find average people anywhere. To be outstanding means leaving the focus group, the good-enough—attitude group. The desire to grow in knowledge, skills, understanding, and self-control is the expression of a man's commitment to the life process, and to the state of being a human being.

Finally, do not aim to be a good brown person, a good white person, a good polka-dot person, a good pinstriped person. Aim universally to be an excellent person. We do not need more fragmentations of white men, black men, yellow men. We simply need human man. Human women. Human citizens who sow good wherever they are because they realize that if we take, and put nothing back, there will be nothing to take.

Pride is inextricably tied to achievement. Without pride in oneself, one's work, it is easy to develop the good-enough attitude or the so-what-it's-not-my-problem attitude. Our productive ambition reflects not only our range of intelligence but, most crucially, the degree of our self-esteem.

Admire others, but become your own hero . . . your own heroine. God gave each of us everything we need to be outstanding; all we need to do is cease looking elsewhere for what lies within us. Decide now, this moment, to amaze the world, to rise above being average. You, too, can have the world's eyes holding wonder like a cup. It is our birthright. Excellence awaits you, don't let it flicker away. Empower your mind. Empower your thoughts. Empower what you give to others, and then you can give yourself the daily hug that I give to myself daily by saying: "I love you, Marva Collins; you are wonderful." To do less than this is truly a sin of omission.

Marva N. Collins

Anna L. Cooke

Author of *The History of Lane College*;
Freelance Writer

Dear Success Seeker . . .

To be successful in life, you must believe in yourself. At an early age, I watched and admired persons who had been successful and tried to analyze how they attained the goals they had set for themselves. I have found through the years that success is measured not only in achievements but in lessons learned, lives touched, and moments shared along the way.

My mother died when I was only five years old. My paternal grandmother came to live with us: my sister, brother, and myself. I was the only one who had the determination to get a higher education. My sister and brother chose early marriage but did rear successful families. I learned from their experience, my neighbors, and my teachers who guided me with encouragement. My religious training helped me to develop strong values in my life.

My favorite books have always been biographies and inspirational ones. I recommend *Conversations,* by Johnnetta B. Cole; *In My Place,* by Charlayne Hunter-Gault; *Having Our Say,* by the Delany

Sisters; *Lessons in Living,* by Susan L. Taylor; and *Splashes Of Joy in the Cesspool Of Life,* by Barbara Johnson.

As you travel life's highway, be yourself—truthfully, accept yourself; gratefully, value yourself; joyfully, trust yourself; confidently, empower yourself—prayerfully; and success will be yours. Always remember—failure does not build character. Do not fear going forward slowly—fear only to stand still.

Sincerely,
Anna L. Cooke

Joan Ganz Cooney

**Creator of *Sesame Street*; Founder of Children's
Television Workshop for Public TV**

Dear Success Seeker . . .

The success I have obtained in my life and career has come from knowledge acquired and applied, experience, and hard work.

The character traits that assisted me the most were:

- desire to excel
- drive
- belief in causes greater than self
- hard work

The books I recommend are:

- *War and Peace*, by Leo Tolstoy
- *Crime and Punishment*, by Fyodor Dostoevsky
- *A Tale of Two Cities*, by Charles Dickens
- *The Age of Innocence*, by Edith Wharton
- *Pride and Prejudice*, by Jane Austen

e whose lives have influenced and motivated me are:

er King Jr.
.coosevelt
- Father James Keller (founder of the Christopher Movement)
- Dorothy Day (founder of the Catholic Worker Movement)

Remember to believe that you *can* succeed if you work hard and avoid the path of least resistance and develop good interpersonal skills.

With my best wishes for your future success,
Joan Ganz Cooney

Barbara Jean Danner

President and Founder, Macon County Fine Arts Manifesto, Inc.; Nationally Renowned Artist

Dear Success Seeker . . .

To have a dream is wonderful; but when you dream and do not accept reality, the dream dies. Reality is accepting rejections, disappointments, and hardships, but allowing the trials and tribulations to be stepping-stones to make your dreams come true. Great people in our country had a dream first, then worked toward the goal of achieving the dream; such as Louis Armstrong, Booker T. Washington, Louis Adams, George Washington Carver, and many more throughout history.

When you are working on a goal, it gets harder as time passes, but I tell my art students to give out but never give up their dream. Everything worthwhile in life starts with a dream. When you put God first to guide you with your dream, the reality will be possible. Always keep your mind focused on the good things in life and leave all negative thoughts behind. This is the beginning to making your dreams possible.

Sincerely,
Barbara J. Danner

Norma Jean Darden

Wilhelmina Model; Owner and Operator of Spoonbread, Inc.

Dear Success Seeker . . .

I've had many careers because I could never decide what I wanted to be. At first I thought about social work, so I started working for the department of welfare. And then I decided retail might be more fascinating, so I went to Bloomingdale's to work. I was in a training program there that prepared me for being a buyer. First I was in the glove department and then towels and linens; but a young man came in one day and said, "You know, you really need to be a model."

Of course at that time I really wanted to be an actress, and I was studying acting. But he said, "Well, you're so tall—first be a model, then go into acting." So I started modeling with Black Beauty, and then I went to the Wilhelmina agency and worked as a model for seven years. I appeared in such magazines as *Essence, Harper's Bazaar,* and *Vogue.* I also went to Europe and worked for several magazines and walked the runway for lots of designers there, as well as in the United States— where I did a lot of television commercials. Then I thought about film, and got small parts in *The Wiz* and *The Cotton Club.*

During the time I was working on *The Cotton Club,* a producer at

Channel 13 asked me to bring some food to a party she was giving. When I brought the food, they liked it so much, they asked me to cater a large party for Channel 13. I didn't know a thing about catering, but my sister and I had just written a cookbook, *Spoonbread and Strawberry Wine.* So my sister and I ended up catering for about two years. It was fun, but then my sister went on to open up her own real estate company, and that left me with the catering business. By this time, so many people were calling me that I just got swamped. And I've had a large catering business ever since.

Catering was a profession that I didn't go looking for, but it found me. Then, of course, once we had the catering business, we opened the first restaurant, Miss Mamie's Spoonbread. That was small, so we opened the second, bigger restaurant, Miss Mamie's Spoonbread Too. The two of them are going nicely, and the catering is still blooming, and the book is still out there.

Although this was not my intended path, it has been successful because it has been what makes me happy. This is how I define success—doing what makes you happy. And hopefully what makes you happy can support you in a lifestyle you find appropriate. My success advice to anyone is to follow your passion, and hopefully your passion will follow you.

For example, lately I did a catering job and met a young man who was a dancer and had lost a leg. So, for most people, that would be the end of a career. But he has worked and gotten his balance back, and he is still dancing. His desire to dance was so strong that he overcame having one leg and found a way to move, because his passion and his desire were so great. And he's still dancing.

You must have confidence in yourself and what you can do with your abilities. And that confidence has to be based on something. So that means to get the best training you can get to do what you want to do.

In closing, you must know yourself, what your assets are, and what your limitations are, so that you can work within that spectrum to be the best that you can possibly be. Be realistic about what it is that you want to do and your ability to do it. Find your niche, and never give up.

Sincerely,
Norma Jean Darden

Patty De Dominic

CEO, PDQ Personnel Services, a Specialized Business Consulting Group; Named Executive Officer of the Year by the *Los Angeles Business Journal*

Dear Success Seeker . . .

How can I best help to guide you through the choppy waters of the next chapter of your work/learning life? Here goes.

Follow your head and *your heart (in about equal balance). Capitalize on your desire to learn, continue your education in and out of school.*

Here are some core skills that I believe will serve you best in the decades to come. Cultivate and refine them to your advantage.

- Resilience
- Flexibility
- Determination
- Tenacity

Create BIG dreams, then live them. Know that all geniuses and successful people (not necessarily synonymous) are wrong sometimes. Don't sweat the small stuff. Money is a benchmark that you can actually define and employ.

I encourage you to determine what you want your destiny to be. Then work hard and smart to achieve it. Grow and be strong. I believe wonderful things will happen to you and others along the way. My wish for you is that you will make our world a better place.

Sincerely,
Patty DeDominic

Ruby Dee

**Award-winning Actress and Author;
Member of Theatre Hall of Fame**

Dear Success Seeker . . .

I believe that no birth is accidental; that each of us comes with a specific purpose to fulfill. The baby's first cry is alerting the elements, is spirit demanding, "Why? Why? Why? How, how, how?" A giggle, a grin, is, "I'm here, I'm here, I'm here."

You are successful if you can arrive at what it is you are supposed to be doing with your life. Sometimes, parents and teachers can help us to arrive at who we are; sometimes we must figure it out ourselves—perhaps through prayer and meditation. Whenever and however we discover this, it is like the jigsaw piece fitting perfectly into the jigsaw puzzle. Perfecting the picture.

Success is when you say yes to yourself—yes, you were supposed to be a mechanic; yes, you are a brick mason; yes, you are a doctor, yes, you are a teacher; yes, you are one who in some way protects society. This is the work that most satisfies your soul, fulfills your purpose here on this earth—work you would do without pay, if necessary. "Yes! I'm a homemaker and I love it!"

The Bible says, "The Kingdom of God is within you." From the lub-dub of Life, the breath we breathe, comes the eternal mantra: "Seek ye first the Kingdom of God . . . all these things will be added unto you." He'll take care of the rent and the food etc., the life and the revelations of its purpose—why you were put here in the first place. I have discovered that nothing is "added unto you" if you cannot use it, or give it, or share it. You must come to the end of your journey having given those things that were "added unto you."

The path to success may bring wealth or fame—or it may not. In the end, it is not about what you have or whom you know. Success is not a static achievement, as listed on a résumé. Success is a changing phenomenon. It may bring unquestionable joy in feeling that the work accomplished is our best—or profound satisfaction as we experience its beneficial effect on the lives of others.

Sincerely,
Ruby Dee

Capucine (Cap) DeLaney

Business Development Manager for
$60 Billion Mass Retailer

Dear Success Seeker . . .

> *In order to have what you have not, you must first do what you have not done.*
>
> —UNKNOWN

It may sound simple, but the above statement has proven to be an invaluable lesson in life that has helped shape my success. Whether interviewing for a job, competing for my next promotion, negotiating a better deal, or seeking to improve relationships, implementing this principle has been the key to achieving my goals.

If you do not have what you desire, ask yourself, "What do I need to go back and focus on in order to have what I want?" In business this is called identifying the "opportunity gap": the difference between what you currently have and what you could potentially have. Do not just sit and wait for things to happen for you. Take the initiative. *"In order to have what you have not, you must first do what you have not done."*

I have seen so many people who want the "finer things in life" but do not want to go through the hard work to get it. They want to acquire possessions and wealth the easy way versus developing the tenacity, patience, and resilience that it takes to obtain assets. Having a successful career entails putting in the required effort. *Remember, anything worth having is worth going through the trouble to get.* Do not be afraid to go through the trouble. Take risks, seek information, and determine your opportunity gaps in order to have the success you desire.

It is important to note that success is not just measured by money and status. Having the courage of your convictions, not giving up even when things do not go as planned, following your passion, learning from your mistakes—these are all examples of success and should be valued as well. *Be sure to celebrate your victories, big or small, along the way.*

Another key to my success has been developing relationships. We have all heard that "it takes a village to raise a child," but it also takes a village to achieve success. Find good mentors (notice that is plural—you can never have too many mentors), establish contacts, and use your resources. This is all a part of building your "team for success" as well as developing your mind with the knowledge, insights, and support supplied by others you know and trust. *Remember, there is strength in numbers; you do not have to do it alone.*

As you continue striving toward success and doing "what you have not done" to get what you want, I share with you the following rules of thumb that will also prove invaluable.

- Learn to accept change—it is the only constant in life.
- If you want something, give it away (want a smile, give a smile; want money, give money; want respect, give respect).
- Integrity, defined as "how you behave when *no one* is watching," is essential to strong character. If nothing else, have integrity.
- Become *and* remain active in your community. Monetary sup-

port is important, but self-involvement is a richer experience.
· Always keep reading and expanding your knowledge. This
helps your growth by increasing your exposure to different
cultures, interests, and ideas.

Last, and most important to my success, has been my family
and God. For me, there is nothing like the bond you hold with
your family and with God. My family has been my confidant, my
support system, my counselor, my comedian (laughter is the spice
of life), my caterer (funny how a homemade meal can lift your
spirits), and much, much more. *Surround yourself with a good support system.*

Having a spiritual connection is extremely important for me.
Hope, faith, prayer, and the belief in a higher power have given me
the strength and courage to battle and overcome anything that comes
my way. It helps make the seemingly impossible possible. It helps keep
me humble, thankful, and appreciative of all the blessings and lessons that He provides. *Have faith in God and you will never falter.*

"In order to have what you have not, you must first do what you have not done"
has been my source of inspiration. I share it with you in hopes that
it lends you some insight to help reach your goals. Nevertheless,
I encourage you to find your own source of inspiration that will
ultimately help shape your success.

I wish you all the best as you continue your personal and professional journeys.

Keep positive influences and pass along your blessings.

Capucine (Cap) DeLaney

Loretta Devine

Award-winning Actress

Dear Success Seeker . . .

It's hard to write a letter about success when you're not feeling successful. Today I'm not. I can hear you saying, "Loretta, with all you have accomplished, how can you say that?" Funny, but you cannot hold success in your hands. Your achievements, your accomplishments, your successes. Intangible, a feeling at best, a feeling. It is not like anger, or fear, or worry. Take a minute and think about it. What did it feel like the last time you succeeded at something? Nice, right? It has colors of pride and joy and satisfaction mixed in it and it feels like winning, right? It's a good feeling, one of the best ones. Right up there with love. Being successful is like an extra skin and an extra layer of protection that gives you power, gets you in, and holds you up.

Today, are you feeling successful?

Being a working actress, I live in the now of everything, or try to, and most of the time I find success and work are one. So today, since my four-year run on *Boston Public* is over and Lifetime just called to say *WildCard* is not being picked up, I am back to square one and I am just not feeling so successful today, but my heart tells me I am. It's another day aboveground. I spend a lot of time hitting the same mark, trying to see if I can keep the ball in the air. Audition after audition after audition after audition and still I see people I've started with rise higher and become wealthier and more famous. I just hope they are having as much fun as I'm having, even today, as I'm feeling like I've got to get on the ball again and find a job or create one. I'm smart enough to know I still have the ball and will get work. Success brings success.

My career has afforded me pleasures that have surpassed my dreams and they keep getting bigger. You must dream big and know each day you may get all you asked for. Each moment is new; enjoy whatever mood you are in and embrace it enough to understand yourself first. Fall in love with your own magnificence and it will be easy to spot it in others. Be successful in your career, your family, and your community, the more the merrier. God bless.

Sincerely,
Loretta Devine

hook her ot

Mimi Donaldson

Author of *Negotiating for Dummies*

Dear Success Seeker . . .

> *"Be bold—and mighty forces will come to your aid."*
> —BASIL KING

This is one of the statements I live by. It is attributed to author Basil King, but I heard Anthony Hopkins quote it on *Inside the Actor's Studio,* one of my favorite television interview shows. Bold is best, and what could be bolder than laughing at life—and while we're at it, all our problems, failings, and foibles? Laughing cuts the big things down to manageable size. So my best advice to you would be to find the "light" part of any situation.

The Failure to Communicate

In this hypertechnological age, for many of us, a face-to-face encounter has come to mean facing a screen. More and more, we are isolating and weakening our people skill muscles. Many of us would rather send an e-mail that takes twenty minutes to carefully compose than have a two-minute telephone conversation. And even the phone is a weak substitute for eyeball-to-eyeball communication.

In my twenty-five years of experience as a corporate consultant, I've learned that a major source of personal stress is the inability to talk to each other and get the result we want. Until we know how to talk to people and gain their cooperation, support, and joy in relationships, we will be stressed. So study communication and practice speaking up appropriately.

Do I Really Have to *Say* That?

Every day, not just once but over and over again, we all have to make courageous choices about what to say. Do we tell the truth to someone who needs to hear it, risking criticism or rejection? And *how* do we say it? And *when* do we say it? Do we keep the truth tucked away inside? If our noses grew like Pinocchio's when we were less than truthful, then this wouldn't be a problem. But that's not the case. We often choose not to say anything, rather than risk discomfort. But silence is not always golden.

Sometimes you need to be bold enough to tell the truth (and this person just might be yourself). Also, you need to be bold enough to resist the urge to say it unkindly. At the end of L. Frank Baum's *Wizard of Oz,* when the Cowardly Lion requests courage, the Wizard tells him he already has it. The Wizard says, "All you need is some visible manifestation so everyone will know you have it."

It's not easy to overcome shyness and fears and speak up. Remember, just because you are scared does not mean you are in danger. Each of us has our own way of slaying the fear dragon. For me, the process has always included humor, even with a lump in my throat. If you can laugh at the dragon, you can make him your pet.

May you be bold and have the courage to communicate.

Mimi Donaldson

Hazel N. Dukes

President of the NAACP New York
State Conference

Dear Success Seeker . . .

Education is important as we make plans for the future. As you know, we go through several stages in preparation for adulthood.

Life is exciting and has many aspects: disappointments, failures, and achievements. An education enables you to seek out how to overcome adversity without becoming discouraged and falling prey to destructive behavior. It teaches us how to search for answers by reading and seeking professional assistance.

If I had not been prepared at an early age on the importance of education, it would have been difficult for me to make it. Being reared in a southern home by God-fearing parents, grandparents, and extended family, I was always told that I could, never that I couldn't. Now, I pass on to you: words from "My Last Will and Testament" by Mary McLeod Bethune.

I leave you love
I leave you hope

I leave you the challenge of developing confidence in one another
I leave you a thirst for education
I leave you a respect for the uses of power
I leave you faith
I leave you racial dignity
I leave you a desire to live harmoniously with your fellow men
I leave you finally a responsibility to our young people

Hazel N. Dukes

Katherine Dunham

**Internationally Acclaimed Dancer
and Choreographer; Recipient of the
Kennedy Center Honors, One of
the Highest Artistic Awards in the United States**

Dear Success Seeker . . .

As a child I was drawn to dance through my passion for the art form, yet dance led to many paths, most notably the then unconventional path of anthropology. Over sixty years ago, I was a young African-American woman venturing into a scientific field dominated by European men. My course, although an exciting and educational journey, was not easy.

As a younger I was very much influenced by my brother, Albert Dunham. Albert, a musician and amateur dramatist, became a noted philosopher. He inspired me to strive for excellence. As a young adult, the person who had a most lasting and all-encompassing impression on me was philosopher Dr. Eric Fromm. I met Dr. Fromm when I was a Rosenwald Fellow about to embark on anthropological research on dance and culture in the Caribbean. He taught me about fighting for one's civil liberties and encouraged me in my life as a researcher, scholar, and cultural activist.

As you venture along your path of discovery and growth, remember to be yourself, be a creative and inventive thinker, and learn from all people and situations around you. Although I have named two people who had exceptional influence on me, the number of people by whom I have been inspired and who have assisted in my growth and development is too large for me to name in this letter, and therefore I say to you to learn from all relative people around you.

With love and great hope, I challenge you to go forth and make a world.

Sincerely yours,
Katherine Dunham

Sheila E.

Drummer and Singer; Musical Director for Jennifer Lopez, Beyoncé Knowles, and Prince

Dear Success Seeker . . .

I've been an entertainer for the majority of my life. My family, being very musical and very active in the community, took center stage at every opportunity. As I recall, regardless of our lower-class status, we were exposed to every level of life. Although we were struggling financially, our parents felt it was their responsibility to take care of anyone in need. We would go to foster homes and perform; my mom would cook for them whenever possible. Whether we performed for the needy or elite, it was important that we planted seeds. We didn't have much, but what we had, we gave. This principle would follow me in every aspect of my life.

In the interim, I was taught that being a team player was essential. My family, including my mother, was very active in sports. Personally, I found interest in athletics in school. I enjoyed soccer and ran track. Was even training to go to the Olympics because of my skills in track and field. How interesting that some

...ndamental tools of life were imparted within me through ...n order to win, it took hard work, but more important, it ...ial to work as a team. Everyone benefited. The attendees were entertained, and the team worked together to succeed. Not to mention, great relationships were made as a result of working together.

However, it took at least thirty years for me to realize that true success comes through prayer. On any level and for everything! Although I didn't finish high school, I convinced myself that I would be fine. I realized very quickly that I missed out on quite a bit. There were many personal factors that orchestrated my dropping out of school. It was easier to give up than to work hard. As a consequence, life was challenging for quite some time.

However, by the Grace of God, He has shown favor in my life and allowed me to not only be blessed through music, and the acclaim that I have received, but to be a blessing. Through my desire to please God, He has given me the will to learn, to grow, to contribute in so many different ways. Success means nothing if it's self-centered. You will never truly succeed if you are doing it for self-gratification. You must give of yourself daily, to others and for their sakes. A higher level of success is reached through knowing that it is not about you. However, with hard work and perseverance to serve others, it's a win-win situation.

I remember performing about over a decade ago and I thought I wouldn't be able to make it. I went through the motions, playing as I did every night. But there was this girl who caught my eye. She seemed to be watching my every move. Not because she was a fan, but I think she wanted to learn. This spoke volumes. Although I was in a position to entertain, I realized that there are those who desire to grow and be educated through the arts. As a woman, she looked at me as a role model, and through my music, I was her mentor. I've learned that music is not just entertainment, but a necessity to function in so many areas. The arts allow us to express ourselves in a creative way that words could not. One can even find femininity in music—as it is graceful, comforting, and even supportive.

We all succeed when we use the gifts that God has given us. They are given to us for one specific reason, to plant seeds in other lives. To allow these seeds to root and produce a harvest of love and kindness, wholeness and edification, is the ultimate reward. It is my responsibility to give through music, through sharing, and through prayer. With these components, we all win!

May my experiences be a blessing to all that are willing to receive.

In His Grace,
Sheila E.

Marian Wright Edelman, JD

Founder of Children's Defense Fund

Dear Success Seeker . . .

My best advice is the advice I gave each of my own sons in a letter on their twenty-first birthdays. Here are some of the lessons from that book:

1. There is no free lunch. Don't feel entitled to anything you don't sweat and struggle for.
2. Set goals and work quietly and systematically toward them.
3. Never work just for money or for power. They won't save your soul or help you sleep at night.
4. Don't be afraid of taking risks or of being criticized.
5. Be honest.
6. Be confident that you can make a difference.
7. Don't ever stop learning and improving your mind.
8. Choose your friends carefully.
9. Be a can-do, will-try person.
10. You are in charge of your own attitude.
11. Remember your roots, your history, and the forbears' shoulders on which you stand.

12. Be reliable. Be faithful. Finish what you start.
13. Always remember that you are never alone.

I believe these are lessons on how to achieve a real measure of success—not on how to make a living, but how to make a life. I wish you great success as you begin your journeys. I am very proud of you.

Sincerely yours,
Marian Wright Edelman

M. Joycelyn Elders, MD

The First Black and Second Woman to Serve as U.S. Surgeon General

Dear Success Seeker . . .

It is very difficult for me to know where to start. I have so many things I would like to share with you and so little space in which to do it. When I was asked to write this letter, I asked myself, "Am I an outstanding woman leader?" and, "Do I really have any advice that is worth sharing?" These questions allowed me the opportunity to quiet my thoughts, look out the window, reflect upon my life, and daydream.

Nothing could replace the nurture and support of my parents. These folks were the first shoulders I stood on to get where I am today. They gave me a sense of pride and a good spiritual foundation. There were also the shoulders of other family members, friends, coworkers, community and church members. These people supported me because I asked them for help when I needed it. There have been many teachers and mentors who have been there to help guide me through my decision-making processes. I will always remember all of the strong shoulders that supported me

orms in my life and helped me firmly until I could
roceed forward.

l ask for help when you need it; your teachers and
ere to help you and guide you through your decision-making process. They all want you to leave school with four
things:

- A voice in your ear so that you will always be able to hear those less fortunate than yourself.
- A vision in your eye that extends much further than you can see.
- A scroll in your hand, which is a good education.
- A song in your heart to carry you through when times get tough.

We develop a dream and make it become a reality through perseverance because the road to success is littered with those who
gave up. You must never measure your worth by your failures, lest
you will always feel worthless. The only time you fail is the last
time you try. I have had many bends in the road, many disappointments, but I never lost sight of my goal.

Best wishes, and much success as you strive to achieve your
goals.

Sincerely,
M. Joycelyn Elders

Myrlie Evers-Williams

First Woman to Chair the NAACP; Named Woman of the Year by *Ms.* Magazine

Dear Success Seeker . . .

I have been asked to advise you on success. That is a broad and thought-provoking request.

Not being sure where to begin, I sit quietly and reflect on recent conversations with a few friends. Many of them have cautioned me to slow down, walk away from the civil rights struggle, and enjoy life. "You have given enough, you have paid your dues," they said. Indeed, I have sat in silence contemplating my next move. Should I rest on my past accomplishments or with renewed energy find new paths to explore? New challenges to pursue? Yes! That is what keeps us truly alive and viable. However, life provides us with the ability to reflect on lessons from the past and assists us in addressing the challenges of today. The process helps us to build a strong foundation for the future. You are a part of that process.

My husband, civil rights leader Medgar Evers, said to me, "Myrlie, isn't there anything you believe in enough to fight for it?" Those words have been a guiding light in my life decisions. I have walked my journey to a point in the road where I understand the pain and the challenges. My attitude is one of standing tall with open arms to meet them all.

Go for it! You are awesome!

Myrlie Evers-Williams

Judith Berry Griffin

President, Pathways to College; Former National President of A Better Chance

Dear Success Seeker . . .

A letter to my Godchild, Who is Standing on the Shoulders of Giants

Dear Joanna:

Your father often uses the expression: "We are all standing on the shoulders of giants." What he means by that, and what this letter is really about, is what it means to have "giants" to stand on. Once upon a time, people you didn't even know gave something important so that you could be who you are. As African-Americans, you and I have many giants to look back on and thank for their bravery and determination, which is allowing us to live as we do today.

Our ancestors did not want to be slaves, and they were brave enough to resist. Later, our parents, grandparents, and great-grandparents did not want to have to sit at the back of the bus, or only be allowed to drink from a water fountain labeled "Colored," or not be able to have a room in a hotel or even stop to eat a meal at a restaurant, or have to walk miles and miles to go to school. They endured much pain and humiliation, and many even lost their lives so that you and I could go to good schools, travel safely and comfortably anywhere in the country, and have interesting careers to choose among. We are obligated to repay their generosity by following their example; our gift to someone else can be a thank-you for the generosity and courage of those who went before us.

We all must remember who we are—to celebrate our own culture, our community, and our family history. This does not mean that we are unkind to those of other racial backgrounds! It just means that we love ourselves, and that we are happy and proud to be who we are. No one will gain if we try to submerge ourselves in the majority culture. If we were to try and do so, just think of all the beauty we would lose!

A few months ago, I began to do some research on my mother's side of my family. My mother's name was Ophelia. I knew that my grandmother had a sister whose name was Mattie Ophelia. What I discovered, after many days of searching, was that my great-grandmother, born a slave in Bolton, Mississippi, in 1850, was also named Ophelia. How moved I was to discover that she had passed on to her daughter, and to her daughter's daughter, the only wealth she had—her beautiful name.

So you see by their work and their example, our "giants" have helped us to be wealthy in every sense of the word. And because we have been given so much, we are able to give much away.

Joanna, remember that you're part of a big family that is standing on big, broad shoulders! You can reach even higher! Believe in yourself—as all of us believe in you.

I can't wait to see what happens next in your life!

With much love,
Aunt Judith

José-Marie Griffiths, PhD

**Dean, School of Information and Library Science,
University of North Carolina at Chapel Hill;
Appointed to the United States National Science Board
by President George W. Bush**

Dear Success Seeker . . .

Over the past three decades, I have had the opportunity to conduct research in areas as diverse as disintegration rates of radioactive materials, economics of information, metadata structures and retrieval algorithms, information user studies, and advanced technological developments. Most recently, I've been privileged to play a role in university administrations and in national and international policymaking. Many different people have influenced my life and life choices.

One of my earliest and most enduring role models was Marie Curie. I read a biography of her when I was about ten years old. She awoke in me what became a lifelong passion for research and discovery. She influenced my decision to major in physics and inspired me to pursue a research career. I remember that both my fifth-grade teacher and classmates were somewhat startled when

I responded to the question, "What do you want to be when you grow up?" with, "I'm going to be a research scientist!" Later, I read Susan Quinn's thoughtful and comprehensive biography, *Marie Curie: A Life,* and recently I discovered Ruth Lewin Sime's biography of another inspiring physicist, *Lise Meitner: A Life in Physics.* These women lived their lives to the fullest—they were passionate in their pursuits, fully vested in multiple roles, valued and nurtured relationships even when those relationships caused them pain or career loss, saw no division between arts and sciences, and they balanced intellectual and spiritual needs. They were the very manifestations of my mother's adage, "if it's worth doing, it's worth doing well."

Success can be defined in an infinite number of ways. There are many pathways leading to success. Regardless of the path you take, there are a number of things you can do to help propel yourselves toward successful careers, relationships, and lives in general.

Recognize that every day is full of learning opportunities. Marie Curie could have lived much of her adult life as a governess. But she chose to spend time each day on her own education in addition to her responsibility for the education of her charges. Listen to others; look around and observe what's going on. Be aware of your world and your role(s) in it. Imagine the possibilities for your future. After all, Einstein said: "Often, imagination is more important than knowledge." Don't be too despondent about what you see as failures—think about what you can learn from them and use your imagination to help you take the next step. If you haven't experienced failure, you can't truly appreciate success. After all, one definition of success is the ability to overcome failure.

Choose a job or lifestyle that gives you satisfaction. If you enjoy or derive satisfaction from what you do, you will address it with enthusiasm and will be energized by it. When I get up every day, I am eager to get to work, spend time with family, meet friends, etc. This doesn't mean that there won't be difficult times, but that I can get through them because I find it worthwhile to do so. Recogn. and celebrate your talents along with others whose talents challenge, reinforce, or complement yours. Hard work does bring its own rewards, especially when you want to work hard. Do not ask others to do more than you are willing to do yourself.

Channel your energies in positive directions. Focus your energy toward your goals and don't let yourself be distracted by things that are unimportant. Pick your battles carefully (you will encounter or initiate some) and make them worthwhile. During the most difficult times of her life—the death of her husband, Pierre, and the later public condemnation of her affair with Paul Langevin, Marie Curie never abandoned her scientific pursuits. Remember that any energy spent on unimportant things is energy that cannot be spent on those that do matter. And never fight for what you don't believe in. The expenditure of negative energies is far more draining than the expenditure of equivalent amounts of positive energies (which reenergize you). ___

Ensure balance in your life. Successful people tend to be successful in a number of areas of their lives—although not necessarily in all areas, or at the same time. Too much focus on one aspect can generate considerable anxiety, particularly when problems are encountered—the stakes become too high. I have had to balance work and family time. To the extent that I can, I minimize taking my work home; if I do work at home, I try to restrict it to a specific room and set limits on the time. Similarly, I set aside specific time for family activities. Try to take time to step back for a while and contemplate your life in all its aspects. Enjoy multiple activities and interests. Focus on those aspects that are important to you—work, family, friends, community, recreation, spirituality, health—whatever they may be. Vacations and time-outs are important—otherwise your life may become so out of balance that your perspective needs adjusting. Help others you associate with care about and seek balance in their lives as well.

e not those who strive to be first; rather, they are the first to strive.
r the success of a larger goal. They can be identified by the clarity of
gth of their actions, and the integrity of their intent.

vish you a "passion for learning," a "learning life,"
anu a "lifetime of imaginings." For as Oliver Wendell Holmes so
eloquently wrote of imagination: "Man's mind, once stretched by
a new idea, never regains its original dimensions." I wish you well
on your journeys through life. You control your own destinies.
Believe in yourselves and carry your passions and compassions
along with you, and you will be successful.

Sincerely,
José-Marie Griffiths

Esperanza Guerrero-Anderson

**President of Milestone Growth Fund, a Venture
Capital Fund; Recipient of the 2008 Hispanic
Businesswoman of the Year Award**

Dear Success Seeker . . .

The lessons I want to share with you are to set high expectations
for your life. Let your imagination, your dreams, and your desires
flow. No one expectation should be beyond your reach if you set
your mind to it. If you have more than one expectation, don't discard any. Play with them, explore them, gather as much information as you can about them. Don't limit yourself: explore, wonder,
and keep your expectations high. The time will come when you
might need to choose one path and you will be better prepared
if you took the time to learn about all your expectations. As the
saying goes: shoot for the moon because even if you miss, you will
land among stars!

Make a life commitment to be the best person you can be. We
are all like diamonds in the rocks, waiting to be exposed. Our
challenge is to devote enough time and energy to know ourselves
and to nurture the best in us. We all have our shortcomings, our

dark side, but if most of our time goes into strengthening our qualities and virtues, in time our weaknesses will be under control. Think of yourself as a beautiful garden. Tend to your flowers and keep the weeds away! People are attracted to wonderful people. As you become the best person you can be, you will find yourself surrounded by good people willing to help you in your road to success.

My best wishes for your success.

Esperanza Guerrero-Anderson

Mother Velma A. Hamilton

**Pastor of King's Chapel Altar of Prayer Temple;
International Radio Ministry**

Dear Success Seeker . . .

> *Ask, and it shall be given you; seek, and ye shall find; knock, and*
> *it shall be opened unto you.*

MATTHEW 7:7

The preparation for success comes with prayers of appreciation
for wisdom, knowledge, and understanding.

A positive intellect will accept challenges to achieve one's goals.
Dedication, consecration, and separations inspire one to accept
promotion with determination.

For success we must focus on: (A) It shall come to pass, (B) I shall
overcome, and (C) The door will open.

Asking develops one's believing and receiving of wisdom. Our
goals must become our objectives to inquire for faith in our
instructions and counseling. This equips us to accept experiences
and learn from failure.

Seeking serves one with gratitude—you are able to admit mistakes and believe your goal is your ultimate reward.

Note of encouragement: We cannot expose all our desires and fulfillments publicly because we fight unseen foes that attack our strength to succeed.

Seeking is to prayerfully meditate on one's desires daily, which will project personal encouragement. This strengthens with stability to withstand pressures of discomfort and builds an empire of knowledge.

Knocking is persevering with consent to achieve in life. The structure of our thought process has to be educated to promote desires of our heart—this gives us Understanding of Purpose. When we adopt Purpose, personal development will open doors and strengthen us to walk into our destiny with this in mind—*with Christ I can do all things.*

> But seek ye first the kingdom of God, and his righteousness; and
> all these things shall be added unto you.
>
> MATTHEW 6:33

Success is one's choice of responsibility that is given by our Lord and Savior Jesus Christ. Man has been given dominion over the earth to achieve heavenly success. With this authorization of opportunity, we have the power to search beyond struggles and envision ourselves complete in the plan designed for our lives.

The ladder of success deals not only with those who have achieved the most, but also with those who accept the *right* choice and are willing to endure with dignity and integrity. Soldiers are called to fight in war. Many die or are wounded for life before the battle is won or accomplished, but their dignity and integrity have given them their reward of services.

We cannot measure success by standards of accomplishments, but only through additions that are credited—honors given by

Divine plan or ordination for our life. Recognition for time served for accomplishments or purpose helps others.

Success achieved is a test of one's ability to complete the responsibility designed for one's life to lead the way for others to follow.

Seek ye first. This is the principle of life to achieve moral integrity to denounce our foes that cause detours in our living.

Success is a fulfilled life that accepts good counseling with a purpose.

Sincerely,

Velma A. Hamilton

Kathryn Harwig, JD

Author of Five Books Published in
English, German, and Dutch

Dear Success Seeker . . .

It has been said that our only true task in life is to become who we already are. Becoming our true and authentic selves is the key to genuine success and happiness in this world. By discovering your gifts and your challenges and then implementing those into the life which best fits you, you will discover your passion and bliss and also aid the world in becoming a better place.

Becoming who you are is a lifelong process. And along each stage of the journey, new interests, talents, and gifts will be revealed. My father emigrated from the Netherlands, coming to a new land with nothing except a desire for freedom. He instilled in me the passion to be the best I could be. As a small girl, one of my gifts was clear intuitive knowledge. But, because I also desired financial success and acclaim, I turned away from that path and went instead to law school.

Life will continue to push you in new directions. Going to law school gave me analytical and verbal skills and the credibility to write and speak. But my intuition continued to prod me to return to the gifts I had known as a child. With the experience of a successful legal career, I was able to teach and train people about intuition as a usable and reliable tool.

Life will continue to surprise you. In my lifetime, I have set many goals. I have attained a law degree, become a partner in a firm, written five books, and been on national television. And yet, it is the small gifts of the day that continue to delight me. Always be flexible. Always be yourself. Always be kind.

Allow the universe to surprise you. Become yourself and you will be a success.

Blessings,
Kathryn Harwig

Martha Hawkins

Owner and Operator, Martha's Place
Restaurant and Catering

Dear Success Seeker . . .

It doesn't matter what background you come from, you hold
the key to your destiny. You have to unlock your mind and heart
to believe and receive God's purpose for you and your life. I dare
you to dream big dreams—to see yourself being and doing what
you want to become in life. The only person who can stop you
is you. There is power in believing in yourself. Whatever we get
out of life, we pay a price for it. You cannot allow anyone to steal
your dreams or visions. Hold on to them for dear life; do not
give in or give up. I can say this with a true conviction, because
of what I have had to go through in life. As a single mother with
four boys, my life was a real struggle. I attempted suicide by taking
an overdose of tranquilizers and was placed in a mental hospital.
Shortly thereafter, I was returned to public housing and welfare.
At the age of thirty-one, my life was extremely bleak. Being an
uneducated black female from an economically disadvantaged
background, I knew that I would face obstacles and barriers. But,
because I believed that God had a purpose and a plan for my life,

I refused to give up. I decided to take charge of my life and fight my way out of poverty. I knew that my faith and commitment to the word of God was the source of my strength, and I refused to give up. I took my Bible, and looked unto the hills, whence I received help. I went back to school, got my GED, and attended Troy State University, in Montgomery, Alabama. I believe if we work hard at what we want in life, we can make it happen. The lives of many people have provided me with such inspiration. The ones that stand out in my mind are Martin Luther King Jr., Fannie Lou Hamer, and Harriet Tubman, because of the sacrifices and struggles that they had to endure. They were willing to pay the price. Believe in prayer and hard work. Having faith and trust in God is the key; the sky is the limit.

Love,
Martha Hawkins

P.S. Please remember that my thoughts and prayers are with you. I wish you well in all of your endeavors.

Dorothy I. Height

Chair and President Emerita of National Council of Negro Women; Author

Dear Success Seeker . . .

As you move forward in your career, I am pleased and honored to share with you some reflections based on a career that encompasses seven decades.

A young woman holding a key position in government wrote me a note following our luncheon meeting together. She thanked me for advising her not to allow her life to be driven by personal ambition. I had not used those exact words, but she got the message I pass on to you. Ambition is essential. But, self-centered, you stand in your own way. You will also accomplish a great deal if you do not worry about who will get the credit. Enjoy the success of others as well as your own.

Know yourself and set career goals worthy of the person you know you are. Even your studies will help you set your goal. The road will not be easy. Success depends upon your stick-to-ittiveness, and the passion with which you pursue your goals. Hold fast!

Each day I am learning, and I urge you to keep abreast and be knowledgeable about what is happening in your community and in the world around you. Make excellence your hall-

raduate student, I gained an understanding of the

of excellence as a proofreader for *The Negro World*, the

Marcus Garvey published.

You are on your own but not alone. There are experienced, successful people ready and willing to whom you can turn on your journey to success. You will find inspiration for the journey as you read and know more about their lives. I find inspiration to achieve against the odds from many such as Eleanor Roosevelt, Rosa Parks, Benjamin E. Mays, and Martin Luther King Jr.

Find a mentor. I was twenty-five when I came under the tutelage of Mary McLeod Bethune, a woman whose faith in God and faith in herself were a guiding force every day, everywhere. There was no way to work closely with her without growing and gaining new insights. She was deeply spiritual and a woman of vision with her feet solidly on the ground. Her motto was, "Leave no one behind."

You have my every good wish for success in your endeavors. That you take the time to read these notes lets it be known that you are well on your journey to success. In the words of the old Negro spiritual, "Don't you let nobody turn you around!"

Sincerely,
Dorothy I. Height

Andrea Herenton

Entrepreneur: Founder of Hip Education, a Creative and Revolutionary Educational Medium

Dear Success Seeker . . .

Do not be afraid to take appropriate risks. Make sure your risks are aligned with what you believe in. Be confident in your decisions, maintaining a positive attitude. You will achieve remarkable success. Life will be full of a myriad of challenges and sometimes your hopes and dreams will seem impossible. Please do not waste time with regrets from the past. Learn from the past, make adjustments, move forward, and don't look back! The seemingly awful things that have happened in your life are just as significant as the good because they all shape the person you are. Hard to believe, but it's all for the good!

On your journey to finding your fulfilling career path I guarantee you will meet individuals that are smarter, better educated, more attractive, with higher test scores, with wealthier parents, and so on. So what! Don't be dismayed. I strongly urge you to think big dreams no matter what your circumstances are because there is phenomenal power in the way you think! Make specific and measurable goals. Be prepared when opportunities present themselves, like having your résumé ready, practicing what you will say, knowing what's appropriate to wear, etc. The perception people have about you can be very real. So make the most of every opportunity. Keep your goals and priorities aligned with your family and faith because it's like determining which is more important—the left wing or the right wing of an airplane. Both are important! Don't allow anyone to place you in a prepackaged box because you are a woman, person of color, or socially disadvantaged. I have the attitude that I was never in a box to begin with (confidence) because I am truly a unique individual like no other.

Lastly, practice and learn the art of listening to your inner soul. You can achieve listening to your inner soul best when you find a quiet, special place to talk to God. Try not to talk to God just for him only to hear you, but most important, talk to the Omnipresent so you can hear what he has to say back to you. Place yourself in a physically and mentally healthy environment. Surround yourself with people who will celebrate your successes and encourage you in your failures. Heed advice from people who are loyal to you, those who genuinely care, and people who are where you want to be. Proverbs says that to a man (or woman) who seeks many advisors, victory is sure. This is your one special and remarkable life. Take ownership in navigating your personal and career development. Reach for the stars . . . and together we will shine in the universe!

Peace, joy, and success,
Andrea Herenton

Betsy D. Holden

Senior Adviser to McKinsey & Company; Former Co-CEO of Kraft Foods and CEO of Kraft Foods North America

Dear Success Seeker . . .

Success takes many forms. It's something that each of us must define for ourself and pursue in our own way. As I look at my career and my personal life, there are a few principles that I've found useful. I hope they'll help you, too.

Find your place. Find something you love to do, something that you have a passion for and gives you a sense of personal fulfillment. Money, status, or what others think shouldn't sway you in your choice of a career. If you can't wait to jump out of bed and go to work, then you're in the right place.

Begin by asking yourself, "What am I good at and what do I love to do?" Keep on asking these questions because your answer may change over time. Then, seek out a variety of experiences that will help you learn and grow in whatever direction you're headed.

Deliver results. At Kraft, as in all successful companies, if you make good on your commitments—if you deliver results, if you build your business *and* develop your people—you get ahead. It's that simple.

Take risks to make your mark. In any field, the truly successful people are those who figure out ways to do things differently—*and better.* Innovation requires leaving our comfort zone and taking risks. You can manage risk if you plan ahead. Imagine what could go wrong and be ready with plans B, C, and D, so you can turn adversity into an even bigger opportunity.

Aim high. It's important to set big, ambitious goals that require you to stretch your talents—and perhaps even change the rules. If you aim high, you will surprise yourself!

Learn to communicate. Whatever your job or career, your ability to speak and write well will be important. Find opportunities to express your thoughts and ideas in ways that educate, energize, and motivate others. Don't ignore the basics, either. The best communication is brief, clear, and simple.

Embrace change. Change is inevitable—and it can be incredibly exciting. Be open to the opportunities that come with change. Mark Twain once said," . . . the person that had took a bull by the tail once had learnt sixty or seventy times as much as the person that hadn't. . . ." We naturally shy away from difficult situations. But if you think about the times in your life when you've learned or grown the most, they were probably times of significant change or tough, challenging circumstances.

Give something back. As Martin Luther King Jr. wrote, "In a real sense, all life is interrelated. . . . We are inevitably our brother's keeper because we are our brother's brother." Regardless of how busy we are, we can each find some way to give back to our families, our communities, and society as a whole by sharing our wealth, talents, and time.

And finally . . .

Live your values. Whether it's your personal life or career, be true to your values and live them through your actions every day. Integrity has been an especially important value to me. When you have integrity, people know they can count on you—what you say and what you do. This kind of credibility and respect must be earned with consistent behavior over time, no matter what the circumstances. Protect and build your integrity; it's an investment in your future success.

Whatever career you choose, I wish you the best of luck, and I hope that your life brings you everything you hope for—and more.

Sincerely,
Betsy D. Holden

Wilhelmina Holladay

Founder and Chairman of the Board, National Museum of Women in the Arts

Dear Success Seeker . . .

There are two quotes that have helped me enormously in my given pursuits.

One is from Calvin Coolidge. "Nothing in the world can take the place of Persistence. Talent will not; nothing is more common than unsuccessful men with talent. Genius will not; unrewarded genius is almost a proverb. Education will not; the world is full of educated derelicts. Persistence and determination alone are omnipotent."

As a wise old saying tells us, "You have not failed until you quit trying."

I hand these on since I feel that they say more than any composed letter I might write.

Warm best wishes.

Sincerely,
Wilhelmina Holladay

Joan Holman

Nationally Acclaimed Internet Expert

Dear Success Seeker . . .

You will find your true mission in life by listening to your inner guidance system, your inner voice, and following that inner direction to play out the life you were meant to live. Not someone else's life, but your life, a life that may have you at center stage or behind the scenes, a life that may seem grandiose, or very humble. Mother Teresa stated that we will be judged not upon what we did, but the love we put into what we did. And I say that if you have to do something you do not love, then put love into whatever you are doing, and eventually you will be doing what you love.

Many times throughout your life you will have to fly blind, and you will have to be like Luke Skywalker in the 1977 movie *Star Wars* Episode IV—*A New Hope*. To be victorious, he had to shut off the controls, i.e., the mechanical mind, and surrender to those intuitive directions that came from his higher self, his spiritual self. To learn how to do this, practice quiet time every day to try to hear that inner voice. You cannot hear it if you constantly immerse yourself in noise and activity.

There is a master plan and there is order in the universe

the surface, there appears to be injustice, and events appear to be random and have neither rhyme nor reason. But I know to the core of my being that there is much more to life than meets the eye, that there is a Creative Intelligence and that Universal Laws rule our lives, our thoughts, our actions. I trust in a Higher Power and have faith in the process, even though life has been very challenging and difficult for me at times.

So far, my greatest accomplishment in life has been dealing with my personal psychology and coming to a place of self-acceptance and self-love and inner peace. At the core we humans feel very inadequate, and those feelings of inadequacy drive us to behaviors that compensate for, or reflect, these inferiority feelings. This is why people become addicts, victims, martyrs, overachievers, and even underachievers (being the best at being worst). That is why many people destroy their lives and cannot accept and enjoy love and true success.

Seek genuine self-esteem as the foundation for an authentic life. Do not hesitate to humble yourself, and be open to counsel and help. I advise everyone to walk the Twelve Steps that are the basis of Alcoholics Anonymous and all of the Twelve-Step programs. Those Twelve Steps are for all people and are the foundation for having a life of honesty, integrity, and freedom. Most people wear a mask and are not truly free. They are slaves to their dysfunctional psychology and the human ego. They are not truly in control, because they have never surrendered to a Higher Power. True freedom is found in humility, self-acceptance, and surrender.

Oprah Winfrey has said she prays every day for divine guidance and to be used as an instrument to bring good to the world. She is focused on service to life. And she has said she sets goals but then surrenders everything to a Higher Power. This is how I live my own life. Remember that life is all about service, and that you need to be willing to be directed to the highest use of your life for good for the community. My motto is, "To make the world a better place, make yourself a better person." Start first with yourself, work on your spiritual and psychological health and wholeness, and then go forward to live an authentic life being who you really are, a "real" self, and not a "phony" self.

May you discover and become your Real Self.

Joan Holman

Theodora G. Jackson

Founding Director of Jamaica Service Program for Older Adults (JSPOA)

Dear Success Seeker . . .

My father's admonition, "See to it that every place you leave is better off for your having been there," has helped me develop beneficial habits, ranging from picking up gum wrappers in the street to making an effort to change circumstances of the homeless. Many American Indian Nations have laws based on the question, "Will this be good for the seventh generation?" Stewardship applies to how well we develop and direct personal talents as well as to how we protect the environment for present and future inhabitants of the planet. Eric Butterworth's book *Discover the Power Within You* and several works of Joseph Campbell have made indelible impressions on my life and work. In *The Power of Myth* Joseph Campbell emphasizes the call to "follow your bliss." Many experiences have taught me the value of pursuing careers that bring joy, personal growth, and fulfillment. I encourage you to seek work for which you have passion, work that, as Dr. Butterworth says, "allows you to outwork who you are."

Honor the Elders. The lives of my parents and grandparents

were demonstrations of "honesty is the best policy" and "treat others as you wish to be treated." Other such valuable lessons are well stated in the book *Having Our Say,* by the Delaney sisters. The Schomburg Library of Nineteenth-Century Black Women Writers contains a wealth of inspiring information provided by women of great wisdom, intelligence, and courage. One of my favorites in that series is *Behind the Scenes: Or, Thirty Years a Slave, and Four Years in the White House,* by Elizabeth Keckley. Writings of Langston Hughes, Phillis Wheatley, Paul Laurence Dunbar, and Howard Thurman have also enhanced my appreciation of the brilliance, courage, and dedication of our ancestors.

So, my friends, learn from trailblazers of the past; live fully in the present; plan for and expect a healthy and wholesome future!

Sincerely,
Theodora G. Jackson

Janie Jasin

Author of *The Littlest Christmas Tree;*
Celebrates Sobriety since 1976

Dear Success Seeker . . .

He told me to hold the flag straight and stand tall on every Memorial Day, Fourth of July, and many other days in between. His mother, Katie, emigrated from Russia; his father, Henry, was born in Germany. He was the oldest of ten and he was my dad. He believed in the free-enterprise system. He sang patriotic songs. He loved the freedom of speech and quoted from the Declaration of Independence. Mom taught me how to dance the Irish jig, laugh often, and pray. Her maiden name was Flanigan. Her father came from Ireland and her mother came from England. These two parents of mine laid the foundation for my belief in success.

It never occurred to me that success wasn't possible. Risks, stepping out, speaking up, dancing, and praying were a way of life. I had no doubt that talent, work, tenacity, love, listening, caring, and prayer wouldn't deliver peace of mind, fun at achieving, and food on the table. Giving taught me that what went out of the front door returned through the back door multiplied one hundredfold.

I wasted this early knowledge and made my own mistakes. An awakening was achieved through the Twelve Steps of AA. I was finally free at thirty-six years of age. Beginning then, and practicing all I had been shown, success took root. The fruits of faith, family, work, friends, and mentors paid off in my personal and professional well-being.

If we are present to others, our presence becomes a gift. They will see your value, respond with eyes, body language, and words, showing that they value you in and of yourself without any desire to own you or control you. You will be seen in value and grow in that presence. It is on this premise that my work and life are practiced.

Be blessed and know that your life's journey of success is possible. There is help and love all around you. Asking for help first and then receiving it is the magic formula. Then take action with a single step. The rest will follow.

With sincere wishes for your success journey,
Janie Jasin

Carolle Jean-Murat, MD, FACOG

Senior Fellow of the American College
of Obstetricians and Gynecologists;
Award-winning Author

Dear Success Seeker . . .

I would like to share some personal insight with you about overcoming obstacles—and the value of role models—on your path to success.

My bio reads: "board-certified obstetrician and gynecologist; lecturer in five languages; columnist; financial health expert on the advisory board to the GE Center for Financial Learning; author of several books; founder of the nonprofit agency Angels for Haiti; and developer of the S.E.T. for Midlife assessment program for Wellness Centers." But I was born into a family of traditional healers in Haiti, the poorest country in the Western Hemisphere, and I grew up in a caste society. Talk about obstacles—no one in my mother's family had even graduated from primary school.

I was "given" to my grandmother in Port-au-Prince at the age of four, when my parents separated and Mother was unable to care for her children. My mother was from Lacoue Mirabeau, where "low class and evil people" lived, according to our society, because Voodoo religion was practiced in her village. The class system was so strong that my Catholic school kicked me out when they learned of my mother's background. One of my challenges as a young girl was trying to deny the merits of my mother and her family. I didn't see her side of the family often, but when I did, they would shower me with love and inspiration.

At one point, when I became ill, Grandma took me to doctors, but none were able to improve my health. My mother, a village healer and midwife, finally insisted on taking me to my grandfather Mirabeau, a well-known indigenous healer. He restored my health, which made a very great impression on me.

I remember a conversation we had before I returned to Port-au-Prince. "Grandpère, maybe I should learn to be a healer like you." He laughed. "You, a mambo, a Voodoo priestess? No way. Your father would rather see you dead. No more of this foolishness. If you want to take care of people and make everyone happy, why don't you go back home and study hard and become a medical doctor? No one in the Murat family has ever passed primary school. Think about it. You would be our first medical doctor. We would be so proud of you." I thought this sounded pretty good since I was becoming very interested in healing. I remember how important the doctors I visited had looked, even though they were all men.

On a daily basis Grandma was a role model about "mindful living," teaching me about natural healing and how important it is to selflessly take care of others. She had a special bag to use to make you feel better. Being in Grandma's care and having experienced firsthand my maternal grandfather's skills as an indigenous healer, I came to understand that healing had emotional, spiritual, mental, and physical components.

And so the die was cast—I was determined to be a doctor. But it was a long road with many obstacles—finances, culture, gender, and even language were roadblocks.

At age twenty, I left Haiti after finishing college. I had just been accepted to the Autonomous University of Guadalajara Medical School, in Mexico, and my heart was heavy about the uncertainty and hard work ahead. Going to Mexico meant that I would need to learn about a different world, a new culture, and another language.

At the time I spoke Haitian and French, the official language of Haiti. Now I needed to learn Spanish. Since my goal was to be accepted into a postgraduate program in the United States, this also meant that I would have to break another language barrier and learn English.

I also had to learn to deal with dead bodies. The first-semester curriculum in medical school included anatomy. The cadaver I shared with several other students was a middle-aged male. The ID plate on his ear had the number 280, so we called him Dos Ochenta, or Number 280.

The first day I saw Dos Ochenta, with no hair, his parted lips revealing mostly broken, blackened teeth, I ran home and had a nightmare that night. I had no problems working with a skeleton or my anatomy books but I had a major fear of dead bodies.

Our first practical exam consisted of forty dead bodies in the amphitheater, each with a little string attached to the part of the body to be identified. There were forty students taking the exam. We were allowed one minute in front of each cadaver, then had to move on to the next one. I had never seen an open body, and there seemed to me to be no correlation between the nice pictures in the anatomy books and the dead bodies in front of me.

I panicked, and I flunked. My grades were so bad that I was given an ultimatum—either I worked extra hours or I would have to drop out of medical school. Special arrangements were made for me to work on Dos Ochenta by myself, in addition to the time that I had to spend working as a team with the other students.

My challenge was to overcome my fear of cadavers or quit medical school. I knew that I had come far, but I had to go deep within myself to find the strength.

I prayed and I cried myself to sleep. The next morning, I knew I had to face Dos Ochenta. When I entered the room, to my horror, there lay the body of a woman—Dos Ochenta had been mistakenly placed in an amphitheater with thirty-seven other plastic-wrapped bodies, and I had to find him by unwrapping and rewrapping each one.

I was ready to pass out—I unwrapped thirty-two cadavers before I finally found him. What kind of horrible personal test was this? Thereafter, I lay awake for many nights with the lights on because every time I closed my eyes, I would see the faces of cadavers coming to life, jumping up, trying to grab me.

It was a struggle, but after we were reunited I forced myself to spend the required time each day alone with Dos Ochenta. One day while seated on a stool with my back turned, suddenly his left hand, which felt like it weighed a ton, hit my back. Surprising myself, I grabbed his hand and said, "Dos Ochenta, you'd better behave or you'll get in trouble."

I stood up, put my book down on the stool, and started dancing around, screaming and crying, because I knew I had finally overcome my fear of cadavers. I was going to make it! When it was finally time to say good-bye to Dos Ochenta, all cut up, still grinning with his bad teeth, it felt like I was leaving behind a friend. He had helped me overcome a potential barrier to my medical career, and my future.

I could horrify and amuse you with many more anecdotes about medical school, but I must come to the point: obstacles are in everyone's path to success—they are challenges that test your character, help clarify your goals, and solidify your determination. May you look at your personal obstacles as blessings, as I do, especially when I remember Dos Ochenta.

Wishing you every success,
Carolle Jean-Murat

Mae C. Jemison, MD

Physician, Engineer, Astronaut;
First Black Woman to Travel
into Outer Space

Dear Success Seeker . . .

You can't and *you have to* are two deadly phrases that are stumbling blocks for many students. These words—when spoken by a person with special influence—can be very damaging by turning you away from heartfelt aspirations and toward ordinary pursuits. This is particularly true when you intend to do something people are not used to seeing folks like you accomplish.

Two things are helpful in this situation: knowing who you intend to be and then finding the courage to be that person despite what negative, disbelieving people say.

I heard these phrases. I remember as a child telling my teacher that I wanted to be a scientist. She didn't think I knew what a scientist was, and out came those dangerous little helpful ideas, accompanied by her retort: "Don't you mean you want to be a nurse?"

I refused to succumb to the weight of those words and to those who had prescribed my life's path through their narrow prism. I intended to be a scientist, someone who discovers that the world around them has adventures and constantly grows.

Why was I able to overcome? Because I had the support of people who believed in me—my family. I was strengthened by their resolve. This helped me to soar beyond the naysayers, carve my own path, and pursue the possibilities life offers.

And so I encourage you to figure out who you intend to be . . . not so much which job you want to have, but what kind of a person you want to be. Travel; meet and work with people. Take on physical challenges; work in natural settings; work with numbers. Do any of these things. Then I urge you to listen to that little voice inside that is rooting for you. Listen to your heart. Find mentors and confidants who will boost you. Surround yourself with a strong network of people whose faith in you is so compelling that it can shatter the force of the "you can't" and "you have to" people.

Remain curious and inquisitive. Open your hearts and minds to new adventures. Remember the excitement you displayed as a child as you began to peel away the layers of life. Maintain that excitement and that enthusiasm. Successful people have an aura of curiosity and derring-do that sets them apart from others.

Read . . . read . . . read. Reading brings knowledge and gives you access to success pathways. Don't be afraid to explore the world around you. Maintain and exhibit integrity. Resist the temptation to go along just to get along. Know who you intend to be each day. Take steps toward being that person.

Be kind to others. Don't spend time trying to figure out how to make people pay for the wrongs they did to you. The more time you spend in that quagmire of misery, the more of your life you waste and give to them.

All of us will face adversity. It's part of life. Regardless of what fate hurls at you, remain true to yourself and your convictions.

This will help you overcome the chorus of people who would block your path with their "you can'ts" and "you have tos."

As I say in my autobiography, *Find Where the Wind Goes: Moments From My Life,* "Life stretches in front of and behind us, made up of the actions we and others took."

Always remember who you intend to be.

Sincerely,
Mae C. Jemison

Edith Irby Jones, MD, FACPPA

**First Black to Graduate with
Doctor of Medicine Degree from the
University of Arkansas School of Medicine;
First Female President of the
National Medical Association**

Dear Success Seeker . . .

Having been born black in America, female, and poor has given me the personal experiences to know the needs and the difficulties of achieving a "place" to correct and/or improve oneself and help others.

I was taught early by an understanding mother that to excel I had to make greater efforts than some others. I was taught by my mother to read, read everything—comedy books, novels, history, geography, about the cultures of my people and other peoples. By the time I was eight years old I had read the works of John Milton, Shakespeare, Socrates, Plato, Pluto, and much of the Bible such that I felt a part of the world and felt I could shape the world after me.

As I became older, teenage, I had the longing desire to meet people in leadership positions. I made occasions where I got to introduce myself and become a part of their world by participating at first on the peripheral and, as I became more informed, a part of the organizations for which they were leaders.

Being reared in Hot Springs, Arkansas, helped me to meet persons from all over the United States who came there to rest, recreate, rejuvenate, and plan for their work. I began to talk like, walk like, sit like, and feel like I was important. I truly learned there no Off Limits signs for those who desired, made the efforts, and brought others along to share "the promised." If you can think it, see it, and work at it, it belongs to you and you can claim it.

Short cuts to a goal can cause you to lose the focus and miss the goal.

To get good for oneself, one must get good for others, if that good is going to be lasting.

Life for me has been wonderful. It is better than *Alice in Wonderland,* for I know what I want for myself and for others. I wish that all could claim their good in life and share with happiness this paradise through which we pass.

Don't give up your dreams. Don't stop part of the way there—keep going; the paths straighten and beauty and success shine to light your paths.

Love and success as you desire.

Sincerely,
Edith Irby Jones

Shirley Jones

Academy Award—winning Actress and Entertainer

Dear Success Seeker . . .

They've asked me to write a "success letter" with some advice on how to achieve it, some "shortcuts," some "formula" that might save you time and struggle on your way to your mountaintop. At first I was hesitant. I never did get behind those generic, rubber-stamp, one-size-fits-all life prescriptions, especially where significant and personal choices are to be made. It crossed my mind that one of your first "life choices" would be wading through the barrel of success roadmaps you'd be getting, and trying to decide which one really fit. And as I slipped into my sympathies for that monumental operation and cautions I would offer you in that delicate process, it suddenly occurred to me that I had stumbled on a pretty damn good generic, rubber-stamp, one-size-could-very-easily-fit-all suggestion for this letter. Let me give it a try:

Gather up all the offerings and just read them. Look to "decide" nothing, "weigh" nothing, "choose" nothing. Just read the words and let your visceral, organic machine tell you what "feels" right; not your head, but your gut. (As seasoned veterans of society's never-ending war on substance addiction, we have come to distrust what merely "feels good" for what's more academically "right" when our body antennas are alone capable of profound and prudent messages we would do well to read.)

Try it now, with all those life submissions. Try the instant "qualification" that will leap out at you with some of the prominent signatures. Discard the fancy rhetoric no matter how impressive, and save only the words that make you smile and grab your bones. Those are the ones that will melt your gates and turn your wheels. And when you've won your God and set your footprints in the Hall of Fame, then you can sit down, have a beer, and tell your brain what happened.

All my love,
Shirley Jones

The Reverend Barbara L. King

Founder and Spiritual Leader of Hillside Chapel and Truth Center, Inc.

Dear Success Seeker . . .

It is always a joy for me to address young people journeying into adulthood. What an exciting time of life, when your visions and dreams are ahead of you and all the successes you are seeking are on their way to being realized.

As the minister and founder of Hillside Chapel and Truth Center, Inc., I have had the opportunity to speak with and counsel many young adults on achieving their goals. It has always given me a golden opportunity to share a formula for success with those that were already experiencing uncertainty about their future. It is a simple formula that never fails and can be used by anyone, at any age, to achieve his or her dreams of success.

The formula for the success and manifestation of your vision and dreams is:

Passion + Visualization + Prayer + Faith + Thanksgiving = Success

Passion is a hunger that blocks out anything or anyone that interferes with your reaching your goal. You must have a powerful passion for whatever it is you desire. A strong passion will empower you and help you overcome obstacles and challenges that are surely going to cross your path.

Visualize yourself as a success. Visualization helps you keep your eyes, mind/body, and spirit on achieving your goal. If you can see it, you can achieve it. Making a chart of exactly what you want or keeping a journal of what you want will help you in times of challenge and difficulty. Quietly meditate and draw on the power of imagination to form a picture of what you desire.

Make God your partner for success. Ask for the guidance and direction you will need to realize your success. Prayer will help you believe in yourself and push the fear of failure behind you. Prayer will help you forgive yourself and others and move on toward your vision. God is just one prayer away and He always answers prayers. "And all things, whatsoever ye shall ask in prayer, believing, ye shall receive" (Matthew 21:22).

Faith is believing that your prayers are heard and will be answered even though you can't see the results. You must constantly remember that GOD NEVER FAILS. When fears and doubts creep in, as they will, that is the time your faith must be its strongest. Go about your business knowing that your Partner is answering your prayers ON TIME.

Take moments throughout the day to give thanks for your smallest blessings. Let God know that you appreciate and are thankful for the blessings you have already received and the ones that have not been revealed to you. Keeping ourselves poised in thanksgiving keeps us ever ready to receive our blessings and success. Thank You, Father; Thank You, Father; Thank You, Father. And so it is.

As a minister of Truth for thirty years, I promise you that if you use the formula for success faithfully each day, your vision and dreams will become a reality. I am humbly grateful that I was invited to share my thoughts on success with you. As you follow your dream, remember: whatever you face in life, don't let God be the last place you turn. Seek God first in all things and enjoy the blessings of success and abundance.

God bless you,
Barbara L. King

Billie Jean King

Tennis Icon (Won 39 Grand Slam Tennis Titles Including a Record Twenty Titles at Wimbledon); Founder of the Women's Tennis Association and the Women's Sports Foundation

Dear Success Seeker . . .

Undoubtedly, life is not a game, it is a process—a process that requires personally defining success, taking risks, and giving your best shot. Continuously strive for excellence and being better today than you were yesterday. Ultimately, this will result in attaining a winning position in life and obtaining valuable experiences.

Life is full of experiences, and experience is priceless. Use your life's experiences to give back and positively impact the lives of others. Use your talents to win, not only for yourself but generations to come. Then, and only then, can you achieve true success.

Based on my life experiences, I believe success is based on character, determination, and ethics. It is so important to do the right thing, keep your word, and take the higher road. As M. Scott Peck wrote, there are four disciplines that play an integral part in our lives:

cept responsibility for your own actions.
2. Dedicate yourself to your truth.
3. Find balance in your life (through family, friends).
4. Delay gratification.

I am also a strong believer that in order to have a successful life:

One needs to personally define success. Success means different things at different times to different people. Find out what success means to you, and begin your quest to achieve it. We need to reinvent ourselves in a daily way. Self-awareness is probably the most important thing toward being a champion.

One has to take risks to achieve huge success. Life is full of challenges and obstacles, but never let this be an excuse for not taking risks. For without taking risks, you can never accomplish your goals. Don't ever let fear or pressure keep you from your dreams. The world is not changed with hype but with results.

What you give is what you get in life. Let your passion and purpose in life—for who you are and what you want to be—lead you to countless opportunities. Let your love and desire to positively impact the world lead you to make history and achieve much success. It is also important, however, to take time out for yourself.

The best of luck in your life and success endeavors.

Sincerely,
Billie Jean King

Reatha Clark King, PhD

**Former President and Board Chair
of the General Mills Foundation; Former
Vice President of General Mills, Inc.**

Dear Success Seeker . . .

It is indeed an honor and a privilege for me to share my thoughts with you. You are my friend because you are learning how to improve your own life. By doing this, you are preparing yourself to be happier and to be able to help other people and communities in the future. I thank you for your interest in what I have to say.

My life has been a marvelous journey every step of the way. Many people have helped me and have traveled the journey with me. So, my first piece of wisdom to share with you is that I have accomplished nothing alone. My careers as a research chemist, educator, philanthropist, and parent have been fascinating, venturesome, and rewarding. The communities in which I have lived have always been a source of education and lifelong learning. Above all, my family has been a source of support and great happiness.

Never in my wildest dreams did I realize how well I would be able to move through my early years of poverty into such blessed and happy years to follow. My experiences have shown me that America really is a land of opportunity. Those who accept opportunity and work hard can overcome barriers to success. They can achieve personal and professional goals and contribute to the success of their families and communities.

Realize that you are a unique and precious human being. You were created to be special. Realize that you have special talents to share with others—your family, your community, and your work colleagues. The more you believe this, the more your talents will be revealed to you and to others.

Commit yourself to service. Have a purpose in life that extends beyond meeting your own needs. Reach out to others and share your resources with others. Just imagine yourself to be a blossoming flower, and realize that flowers rarely blossom by turning their petals "inward." As a bud blooms, it opens up. Others around the bud provide the space for it to open up, and then they enjoy the beauty of the flower. The same will happen to you as you open up and reach out to others. My wisdom to you is to commit yourself to service to your employer, your community, and your family. Think of yourself as a blossoming flower all of the time.

Have faith and believe that problems can and will be solved! Be willing to learn from all situations and all people, regardless of the other person's race, age, and gender. A person's race is a beautiful thing, regardless of the skin color. Show your magic by your willingness to embrace others and to learn from them.

Second, make education and lifelong learning a personal passion that you do for work and for enjoyment. Open up your world by reading and traveling, and through inspirational quotes by others who have paved the way for your success. For sure, reading and traveling expand our horizons and help us break down our myths about other people and their cultures. Adopt role models and think of them on your rough days.

As you use this wisdom from my life, I want you to keep in mind that you are a beautiful creature and that, if you try, you will be a successful and happy person. It has been a great pleasure to share these thoughts with you, and I wish you great joy on your journey in life!

Sincerely,
Reatha Clark King

Deborah M. Kolb, PhD

**Professor; Author of *The Shadow Negotiation*,
One of *Harvard Business Review*'s
Ten Best Business Books of 2000**

Dear Success Seeker . . .

Lots of people think negotiation is something that happens when they buy a car or when sports stars hold out for big salaries to play ball. But money doesn't have to change hands for negotiation to take place. Every day we negotiate about our work and our relationships. Every day we negotiate opportunities for the future. Sometimes we deliberately direct the process; other times, it takes place without us noticing. A group of friends wants to go to the movies. Several trailers look promising. Where they end up for the evening is the result of a mini-negotiation. A prize assignment is up for grabs, an adviser is skeptical about a senior project, you are doing the work of two but being paid for one, the athletic department won't spring for uniforms for the girls' hockey team, the boss gives you a mediocre performance review—each is a decision just waiting to be negotiated.

These discrete negotiations—the little ones as well as the big ones—create the patterns of a life. Negotiation, in fact, is a prime means of working through conflict and putting your stamp on change. It is a way of changing things for you and for other people. Every outcome you negotiate involves a choice, but first you have to recognize that choice is possible. Flattered to be asked to take on a big project, you don't negotiate for the resources you will need to be successful. That is a choice. What you get (or don't get) in these situations rests in part on your decision to negotiate or not. The more conscious you are of the possibilities for negotiating, the more confidence you will have and the more control you will have over the results.

Negotiable moments, in fact, give you a platform—a time to find your voice and create opportunities. All too often people let these moments pass. You have a great idea for a volunteer project, but the administration vetoes it. If you accept no, your great idea may never be realized. The value of the work you do or can do disappears from view unless you claim it. When a woman's work disappears, so does her influence.

For many years I have talked to women about their negotiating experiences and the challenges they face. We've learned a lot from them that is not covered in the popular books on negotiation. We've learned that sometimes women can be their own worst enemy when it comes to negotiation. Afraid of stepping on other people's toes, they can forget to stick up for themselves. Sometimes they don't want to cause friction and settle for less just to keep the peace. Sometimes they focus on what's wrong, at the expense of all that they have going for them. So the first step in negotiation is to stay out of your own way, to recognize the unique talents and value you bring to a situation. The second big step is to figure out where you want to go. You won't be able to get what you want unless you know what you want. Without that clarity, it is easier for others to control the agenda. Finally, the more information you have about the situation—what other people have achieved—the more confident you will feel. You need to become an advocate for what you want. You can't expect others to do it for you.

With clear goals in mind and information to back them up, you feel confident. You know there is value in what you have to say. But getting in a good position to negotiate is only part of what you need to do. The best negotiations are not battles where people argue for what they want. They happen when the people involved work together to come up with solutions that meet their mutual needs.

A negotiation is not only an opportunity to find your own voice; it is a chance to let the other person be heard as well. He or she probably sees the problem very differently than you do. You need to appreciate that perspective. Show that you are interested in what he or she has to say and try really hard to hear what is said. Consider ideas, even those that seem strange. You would be surprised at how people respond when they think you care about their opinions. When you build trust with the other person, negotiation can become not just a way to resolve a particular problem but a learning experience—for both sides.

I've talked to many women who were unbelievably good negotiators. Each had her personal style of negotiation but all managed to do two things: find their own voice and make room for the other person's to be heard. If you can successfully advocate for yourself so the other person really understands what you need, and if you can connect with them, you are poised to work out problems in a constructive way. You won't be afraid of sticking up for yourself because you will know that good things will come of it. And the other person won't be afraid to meet you halfway because he or she will know that the communication goes two ways. Negotiators who trust each other can probe deeper, more candidly, and the prospects for good solutions increase exponentially. And part of your job as a negotiator is to build mutual respect.

How you negotiate influences the shape your life will take.

There are opportunities waiting to be negotiated. When we negotiate purposefully not to overpower the other person but to establish our voice, we lay the groundwork for mutual respect. In a complex and rapidly changing world, no one can have all the answers. The possibility of dialogue, the opportunity to create one, to benefit from other viewpoints, other people's skills—this is part of the promise of everyday negotiation. It can empower all who participate.

May you find an authentic voice to negotiate for the life you want.

Deborah M. Kolb

Patti LaBelle

Grammy and American Music
Award–winning Singer and Entertainer

Dear Success Seeker . . .

Believe what you know in your heart. Think about *American Idol*. If those finalists had listened to every criticism that was thrown at them, some of them might not have made it as far as they did.

If you know in your heart what your dream is, keep it your dream. Don't let anyone take that away from you.

And, sometimes you don't have to tell people what your dreams are, because people are always ready to bring you down with them. They'll tell you "you'll never make it" or "you'll have to work so much harder." And, they'll say it's because you're black, or because you're a woman.

Don't evaluate yourself based on other people's standards. I'm successful to *my* standards, and it's because I'm doing my best—by being *myself.*

Do what you do, and whatever comes, comes.

And don't do things based solely on money. It's not always about the money, or the Grammy. I have the respect of the public. You can't buy what I have; you can't be nominated for it. Be true to yourself.

Patti LaBelle

Senator Mary L. Landrieu

U.S. Senator

Dear Success Seeker . . .

If you ask a thousand different people what success is, you will almost certainly get a thousand different answers. The word typically conjures up mental images of enormous wealth and power, big homes, expensive cars, luxury vacations. To many of us, these things are part of the picture of success, but only a small part of it.

By the time we become adults, most of us have our own personal concept of success—often developed through trial and error as we discover that the trappings of success do not always lead to personal happiness. True success might mean becoming the first person in your family to graduate from college, saving enough money for a down payment on your first home, or being able to provide the things your family needs. For young mothers, it might mean landing a job that will help them become financially independent. For the children of famous actors and performers, success might mean being recognized for their own talents. For struggling immigrants, success could be providing a future for their children. The possibilities are endless, shaped by our individual life experiences and dreams.

I grew up in a politically active family. My father was the mayor of New Orleans, and I watched him work as a pubic servant, making decisions every day that helped people and influenced their lives. I knew early on that I, too, wanted a life in public service. For me, this is part of my definition of success: helping to shape the laws and policies that will make a positive difference in the world around me. First I had to complete my education, and I am grateful for some wonderful teachers and professors who were successful in preparing me and other students to meet our goals in life.

I think it helped to decide what I wanted to do with my life at such a young age, and then focus all of my efforts on that goal. I was elected to the Louisiana legislature shortly after graduating from LSU, when I was just twenty-three years old. There were people who thought I was too young, there were people who thought I would not be taken seriously as a woman. But part of success comes from believing in yourself—and I am so appreciative of the family members and friends who stood by my side when things were tough.

As each of you shapes your hopes and dreams—and forms your own definitions of success—I wish you well. I hope you will not let stumbling blocks become permanent obstacles. I hope you'll surround yourselves with people who will encourage you to be your best. And finally, I encourage you to build on small successes so even when you do not start at the very top, you eventually get there.

Mary L. Landrieu

Brenda Laurel, PhD

Cofounder of Purple Moon, a Company Dedicated to Producing Software and Other Interactive Media Targeted at Preteen Girls

Dear Success Seeker . . .

Success is not as material as you may have been led to think. The promise of America is that we may earn an honest wage for a job well done. Learning to measure success in terms of happiness and well-being rather than personal wealth has been a key to self-worth for me. Of course, we always think we can do better—and we are usually right in that judgment. A healthy person grows, learns, and changes throughout life. But a sense of self-worth serves as the healthy base from which we can venture and achieve great things. Self-worth is immeasurably more important than net worth.

I have found honesty—both with oneself and with others—to be a pivotal character trait. Without it, other virtues cannot be fully realized. Reaching aspirational goals requires that you visualize them clearly. Be willing to make changes along the way in response to what you learn. When a task seems overwhelming, narrow your view and do the next thing. Listen well and speak clearly. You can only find your voice by using it. Push aside anger, indignation, and other negative feelings in order to articulate the positive. When you speak about a problem, include ideas about how to change things. Honor and tell stories. Always look for common ground. A sense of harmony and balance is achievable, even when all is not right with the world. Finding a balanced place within yourself will provide you with great strength and endurance. Integrity begins with having all the parts of you in balance.

The world is full of inspirational people. Jane Goodall, Barry Lopez, and Lynn Margulis are personal heroes for me because of their involvement with the living world and the understanding their work conveys about our relationships with all beings. People who volunteer their time to help others inspire me. People who do their jobs well inspire me; like the nurses who take care of my mother as she suffers with Alzheimer's disease, who demonstrate great skill, effort, and kindness. People who speak out or take political action despite personal risk are my heroes. My children inspire me with their awareness of others and their commitment to making the world a better place.

Wishing you all the best,
Brenda Laurel

Wilma Mankiller

First Woman Elected Principal Chief
of the Cherokee Nation

Dear Success Seeker . . .

   As women search for a shared model of gender equity, we may want to consider some indigenous societies. In Cherokee traditional culture, it was believed that the world existed in a precarious balance and that only right or correct actions maintained that balance. An important part of the balance was equity between men and women. Women were consulted in matters of importance to the community, the clan, the family, and the nation. When a man married a woman, he took up residence with the clan of his wife. We trace our clan ancestry through women. There was a women's council composed of women of each of the seven Cherokee clans. Female warriors called War Women or Pretty Women were tribal dignitaries. There was a belief that the Great Spirit sent messages through women. A woman's power was considered so great that special women were able to declare whether punishment or pardon was to be inflicted.

   In the eighteenth century, one of our Cherokee chiefs, astonished at the absence of women in delegations of colonial negotiators, asked, "Where are your women?" As we move forward into this century with faith, hope, and optimism, we must all ask that question again and again until the truthful answer can be, "Women are everywhere they want to be."

Wilma Mankiller

Patricia McGraw, PhD

First Black Professor at the University of Arkansas, Little Rock (UALR)

Dear Success Seeker . . .

My son, my daughter, I greet you in the manner in which I have addressed my students and young persons throughout my adult life because it is my belief that each boy and girl, of all nationalities, ethnicities, creeds, and colors, whose paths I have crossed, are mine. I claim you as my own to nurture, teach, and guide, for this mission has been bestowed upon me by One who knows all things, and thus prepares us for our purpose while we tarry here upon the earth. This kinship is a mighty one, for it gives me certain keen responsibilities which are evident by the values that I wish to instill in you as future leaders, future mothers and fathers, who must guide and protect our world for others who will follow in generations to come. Because I have been entrusted with the responsibility of providing advice and, hopefully, wisdom, so that your journey down life's path may be made easier, there are particular aspects that ought to be taken into consideration.

You must respect knowledge and its acquisition. Know that to study and to strive for excellence in your educational endeavors is perhaps your best gift to your parents and to the world. Learn to care about answers and inquiries which delve deeply into problems that deal with life pursuits, scientific research, analytical theories, and cultural similarities and differences. Wonder about things! Search for answers to questions that you ponder simply because you wish to know. Do not wait for others to stimulate or to motivate you! Take those on as your own innate responsibility to yourself. *Want to know because it makes you feel good when you find the answer!* This you owe to yourself as an interested student. Respect yourself and your people enough to learn as much as you can about Everything. Your intellectual challenges will be many, but you can handle them if you learn to prepare yourself. Others may attempt to instruct you, but generally, the acquisition of it is mainly up to you, and your own interest and effort.

I was read to before I was born, according to my mother; also, classical music was played for my pleasure while I was in the womb. I did the same for my children, thus following in my parent's footsteps. Frederick Douglass, the great statesman and advocate for freedom, said that you cannot enslave a man who can read and write. You see, he knew what many of us have yet to learn: reading is the key. There is no subject about which one cannot learn if he or she chooses. When I was a girl, growing up in Little Rock, I was not allowed to use the main library downtown; instead, there was a neighborhood library with few books and little else for the "Colored" population. From the first to the sixth grade, the texts we used in class were all hand-me-down ones that the white schools had discarded. I remember very distinctly that there were always names already in each book before I received it. Sometimes the data within were antiquated, but still we read them and learned in spite of the injustice. We knew that we were indeed standing on the sacred ground of our ancestors who were not even allowed to learn to read and to write, so we studied and we grew, spiritually, culturally, intellectually, to become who we are today. I was a high school graduate at age fifteen, a college graduate at age nineteen, and am now a holder of a BA, MA, and a PhD degree from several major universities in the United States.

Know that you are blessed and that you are loved.

Yours affectionately,
Patricia McGraw

Joyce Meyer

New York Times Bestselling Author;
World-leading Practical Bible Teacher

Dear Success Seeker . . .

If anyone had an excuse to give up and do nothing with her life, I did. I was abused as a child, had a disastrous first marriage, and had every excuse to live in guilt and anger for the rest of my life. But thank God I didn't stay in those excuses.

So why didn't I? Why did I become successful? The first step in being successful is to trust God. The Bible tells us that God has incredible plans for us, but we have to accept Him into our lives for those plans to begin. We were created for His glory, and until we allow Him to be glorified through us, we will never truly be successful. We may accomplish some things, have a measure of material wealth, but we will never be truly happy and blessed until we realize and accept that Christ died to give us life, and life abundantly.

I have also learned over the years that if you want to be successful, you have to give. It is a principle found throughout the Bible, and it has worked in my life. You must give of your time, your effort, your love, your money; you must put others first and honor

God with your life, and He will promote you. God has incredible plans for all people, but it is up to us if we will allow those plans to operate in our lives. We can choose to do everything in our own strength, and we may see a small measure of success in what we do. But when we let go and let God and allow our lives to be used by Him, there are no limits on what we can accomplish.

You may have picked up this book looking for a three-step plan to success, or the top ten traits of successful people. This is the real world. There is no quick fix, just a lifetime of work ahead. But when your efforts are combined with God's blessings, there is nothing that you cannot accomplish, and there is no one you cannot reach. There is no other way of life that will give you the joy to actually appreciate your success.

Your success depends upon your choice. Will you cling to the little success you can accomplish in your own strength, or will you allow God to work in your life, and allow Him to remove the limits on what your life can accomplish?

Sincerely,
Joyce Meyer

Mo'Nique

Award-winning Comedienne and Actress

Dear Success Seeker . . .

    I can't say that I ever had a plan B, but I always knew that I wanted to be a Star. When I moved here to Los Angeles, my goal was to become a Star, and it was as simple as that. I would *never* let anyone tell me that I couldn't make it. To be successful is truly a mental thing. Set your mind to it and then do it.

Mo'Nique

Betty J. Overton-Adkins, PhD

Vice President of Academic Affairs
at Spring Arbor University

Dear Success Seeker . . .

I send you greetings and best wishes. I have high hopes for your future, the future of our country and world. Despite acts of terrorism, bigotry, and hatred, you must believe that most people are basically good. Failure to acknowledge that goodness will cause you to approach the world with a sense of fear, pessimism, and caution. Success for you will come from seeing more opportunities than threats, recognizing your fears but moving forward despite them, and expecting life will turn out well. This type of thinking isn't foolish. It is powerful, affirming, and therapeutic. It causes you to see potential in others, and for them to see it in you.

Optimism and positive attitude are only two ways of achieving success. Another is setting goals. If you are to be successful, you must have goals. Your goals don't have to be earthshaking, but they need to inspire you and move you to work. Your success can be equally measured by your pursuit of your goals as well as by the accomplishment of your goals. Failure comes not because we don't reach our goals but because we flounder in halfhearted

means you must not be afraid of work, struggle,
these are necessary ingredients and by-products of

remember that ultimately success is not about money,
power, or prestige. These things in and of themselves
are not good or bad. Your use of them will define their value.
Your highest success should come from knowing God, serving
people, and loving yourself.

I wish you well.

Betty J. Overton-Adkins

Rosa Parks

Mother of the Modern Day Civil Rights Movement (1955–1968); Cofounder, the Rosa and Raymond Parks Institute for Self Development

---

The Rosa and Raymond Parks Institute for Self Development (Detroit, Michigan) is committed to helping preserve and continue Rosa Parks's life work! Cofounded in February 1987 by Mrs. Rosa Parks and Ms. Elaine Eason Steele, in honor of Raymond Parks (1903–1977), the Rosa and Raymond Parks Institute for Self Development is the living legacy of two individuals who committed their lives to civil and human rights. Both Raymond and Rosa were committed to encouraging others to register to vote, pool their financial resources, advocate for quality formal education, and become involved in community development. The Rosa and Raymond Parks Institute for Self Development is wholeheartedly devoted to and supportive of the legacy organization that Mrs. Parks established and loved.

Dear Success Seeker . . .

At eighty-nine years of age, it continues to be my life's work to encourage all young people to be successful. Success is knowing that we are all leaders of something in life. Each young person should be assured they are a leader. My message to all "success seekers" is work hard, and in everything you do, try to do your best, complete your education, and maintain high moral standards.

Sincerely,
Rosa Parks

Phylicia Rashad

Award-winning Actress; First Black Woman to Win Leading Actress Tony Award

Dear Success Seeker . . .

I suppose there are as many formulae for success as there are people who would develop them. Mine is quite simple: I found that I achieved success in my career when I understood my work to be an offering to humanity and approached it in that way. I've come to believe that this is true of all endeavors. This doesn't mean that you won't get paid for your efforts. This doesn't mean that you don't approach your work in a businesslike manner. What it does mean is the foremost thought in your heart and mind is to offer something of value to people because *you* value people.

Phylicia Rashad

Della Reese

Award-winning Actress and Singer;
Recipient of Hollywood Walk of Fame Star;
Ordained Minister, UP Church

Dear Success Seeker . . .

God has blessed me to be successful and I could really end this letter right here because what I have used was all that I had, and all that I had was my belief in God.

My mother scrubbed floors and my father poured steel. I was born in the slums. I didn't have any connections. I didn't have any sponsor. But God had given me this talent and had also given me the desire to do whatever would meet with His approval that would help me to succeed. This gave me the courage to step out when there was no firm ground. This gave me the incentive to continue toward my goal.

All I can offer you is the same God that I used and tell you that I am a living witness that if you will trust Him, obey Him, and use what you have, you can get what you want.

Lovingly,
Della Reese

Julieanna L. Richardson, JD

Historian; Founder of *The HistoryMakers*

Dear Success Seeker . . .

I am honored to be asked to be a part of this project. When thinking about what makes a person successful, for me it was being born of a father and mother who gave me a wonderful foundation from which I could launch. I learned very early the importance and value of work. Work has been essential to any success that I have achieved, but I must say that for people seeking to be successful, the end result is often not as important as the journey—for life is a journey. One that is full of surprises, disappointments, and challenges.

I started my career very interested in the theater, almost exclusively so. This was before I went on to earn my law degree. In July 1999, I founded a national video archival initiative, *The HistoryMakers*. It is with this project where I have found my place in life. While I am committed to building a one-of-a-kind archive of *HistoryMakers* both well known and unsung that will be enjoyed for generations to come, my journey has not been easy. It is one that took me from Brandeis University to Harvard Law School; from corporate law to city government; from owner of a home shopping channel to the cable industry. It has been a journey and a fascinating one at that.

Enjoy your journey.

Sincerely,
Julieanna L. Richardson

Patricia Turner Robinson

Former Director of Community Relations, Blue Cross/Blue Shield of Louisiana

Dear Success Seeker . . .

I have been employed in the insurance industry for the past twenty-eight years. During my tenure, several of my mentors gave me quotes to live by during times of change. I would like to share some of those with you so they can enrich your life as they have mine.

If Life Gives You Lemons, Make Lemonade

Have you ever been discouraged to the point of wanting to give up? Have you wondered "why me?" Have you felt that you did everything correct or to the best of your ability and the outcome wasn't fair? Have you watched others breeze by you, climbing the corporate ladder with ease? Have you ever felt as though the corporate ladder was greased for you and you began to slide down? Have you been in situations where you received 99 percent support and 1 percent adversity, but the adversary won a few rounds? My advice is, "Never let them see you sweat!" You should have at least one person confident about you 100 percent of the time, and that's you!

Winning Isn't Everything, But the Effort to Win Is!

Having direction in life is very motivational. Knowing what you have to do to get where you want to be is fulfilling. The process of getting there is designed to stretch you beyond normal existence. It is a process of separating those who "want to be" from the doers. You exceed expectations all along your route. You increase awareness of your skills to all observers. Bystanders are in awe, competitors stand with you as equals because . . . there is one winner. The effort is a good example for others, so the competition increases with the next round. Most agree, winning isn't everything, but the effort to win is.

Always Have a Plan B

There is safety in numbers, but have you thought about traveling down the road less traveled? There is a lot to discover, you know. There isn't much "new" on the beaten path. There is safety in numbers, but there is also a lot of competition. In fact, it is so crowded, it is hard to stand out. If you find yourself in an uncomfortable or unfamiliar situation, gather as much information as you can, weigh your options, and select the best course of action. Prepare for change. And, always have a plan B.

Don't give up on your journey to success!

Sincerely,
Patricia Turner Robinson

Mona Lisa Saloy

Folklorist: Author of the Award-winning
Red Beans And Ricely Yours: Poems

Dear Success Seeker . . .

As a young girl growing up in a working-class New Orleans neighborhood, where generations lived and shared a playground, I learned to swim at five; and by twelve, I was an Olympic hopeful. But the onslaught of Civil Rights came late, and I was never able to make my dream of swimming for the USA real.

Because my mother died while I was just a teen, I found myself in the Northwest, attending college aimlessly until I married an ambitious swimmer who aspired to a life in the law. Six months after we were married, returning from a road trip to California, our car rolled over three times and fell thirty feet over an embankment onto the freeway. This accident left me with no memory, a broken pelvis, and a lot of trauma. For a long time, I was flat on my back, then the slow recovery to walking, avoiding stairs, public transportation, or any chance of reinjury. It was then that I wrote to remember; and after having met a few young poets at a coffee shop next door to our apartment building, I was told that I was a writer. These young poets sent me to a writer, Colleen McElroy, who became my mentor, my professor, my friend. Before I left undergraduate school at the University of Washington, I was a professional writer, having won awards publishing in journals, and interning at the University of Washington Press.

I learned that everything that happens to us in life makes us strong or breaks us; that when we learn to lean with the wind, we will bounce straight up like a tree. In this way, we are made stronger by having gone through what life must teach us. We must have faith in ourselves, in God, and in the goodness of life. We breathe each day, don't we? Embrace life. Give thanks for all your blessings, work hard, and life will reward you tremendously.

Now, my students send young writers to me. The cycle continues; that's the way goodness works. Count your blessings. Each one teach one, and pass the goodness.

Red Beans and Ricely Yours,
Mona Lisa Saloy

Lauranne Sams, PhD

**Founder and First President, National
Black Nurses Association; Former Dean of
Tuskegee University School of Nursing**

Dear Success Seeker . . .

When the National Black Nurses Association (NBNA) met for the first time, we met to determine what our directions would be in improving things for our people and making a difference in their lives. At our meetings, each person had the opportunity to talk about how we should be established. But first of all, we wanted to look at what our people needed from us the most.

We looked at what was going on in our country and in our world, and that helped us to know what direction we should go, and what we should be able to do. We knew it would be a large task, but we also knew that we could do it if we took it one step at a time. At that first meeting, we knew we had to eventually have a place of our own. Everybody agreed that each person, once we found a place, would have to contribute. And many did. It was incredible how many people understood and really wanted to make our association a reality.

Today, the NBNA is still thriving, so it must have been important and people must have understood where we were going. Today our objectives are continually evolving, but our main goal remains constant. We have to look at what's happening in our world. We have to look at what's happening in our neighborhoods. We have to look at what's happening to our children. We have to look at what's happening tomorrow. Somebody asked me recently, "When is that organization that you started going to be over?" I say to you, as I said to them, "Never!"

Forever,
Lauranne Sams

P.S. As you pursue success, feel that you are also helping those people who happen to be of a different race/culture to understand you, and to recognize you. Hopefully, someday all people will do those things which are truly needed.

Linda S. Sanford

Senior Vice President, IBM's Enterprise On Demand Transformation & Information Technology

Dear Success Seeker . . .

Family farms are a dwindling piece of the American landscape, which is a shame because you absorb a lot of valuable lessons about life as a kid on a farm. I had the good fortune of growing up in a big family on a potato farm on eastern Long Island. While my own journey has taken me far from the furrowed fields of my youth, I carry with me a few deeply ingrained beliefs I learned on the farm about what it takes to be successful, no matter what avocation you pursue.

Let me describe a few of these traits for your consideration as you begin to carve your own path to success.

First, you must get dirt under your fingernails. In other words, get close to the action. There's no better way to understand the job that needs doing than to do it. Whether it's plowing a field, picking cucumbers, or loading a truckload of potatoes, farming requires rolling up your sleeves and getting the work done. The same holds true in the business world, in the laboratory, and in the courtroom. The most successful people don't leave the hard work and the thorny details to others. The leaders pitch in and take action. They take initiative, set high goals, and don't shy away from whatever hard work it takes to reach their objective.

Living on a 150-acre farm, there was always plenty to do, and most tasks couldn't be accomplished alone. My sisters and I would work together to lift irrigation pipes and move them from one row on a field to another or take turns driving the tractor while others would load the flatbed with potatoes. You had to work as a unit or the day's work would not be completed. In almost every avocation, being able to work as part of a team, to earn the respect of your colleagues and motivate them to bring out their best, is essential for leadership. It's never too early to start developing this skill.

There's a good deal of wisdom in the old saying that luck is what happens when preparation meets opportunity. In farming, a good harvest season never happens through good fortune alone. It's the results of months of careful planning and hard work to plant, nurture, and cultivate a crop. In every walk of life, the people at the top of the ladder are the ones who prepare the hardest. Arthur Rubinstein, the great pianist, once said: "If I miss one day of practice, I notice the difference. If I miss two days of practice, the critics notice the difference. If I miss three days of practice, the audience notices the difference." My point is, to be successful, it may help to be lucky, but what matters most is being prepared. Do your homework.

In farming, adversity comes with the territory. Droughts, floods, blights, bugs, and volatile commodities pricing all add up to a life with no guarantees. There are always setbacks and disappointments. But to some degree, that's true in every field of endeavor. There are always going to be problems and obstacles. Thomas Edison was once asked how he could push ahead having had thousands of experiments fail. He said, "I have not failed. I've just found 10,000 ways that won't work." That's the way the most successful people think. They don't see failure as failure. They view it as part of a learning process that makes them stronger, better, and more determined.

Getting your fingernails dirty, working as a team, and always doing your best to prepare—whether you're farming the north forty or running a Fortune 500 company—will help you harvest a bright future. Remember, the world belongs to the enthusiastic, so go for it!

Sincerely,
Linda S. Sanford

Patricia S. Schroeder

President and CEO of the Association of American Publishers (AAP); Former Senior Woman in U.S. Congress

Dear Success Seeker . . .

The successes I have achieved in my life, and continue to attain, are due, in part, to my strong desire to make a difference. It's important not only to think of the things you want to accomplish but to go out and do it.

I believe you are only as good as your word. Character and integrity are key if you want people to trust you. You must know what you are talking about.

The people who have influenced me and motivated me are my parents and teachers, Eleanor Roosevelt, Amelia Earhart, and Jack and Bobby Kennedy.

I hope you will one day consider running for president of the United States. So set your goals high and have trust in yourself to meet them.

Sincerely,
Patricia S. Schroeder

Cindy Brinker Simmons

President, Levenson & Brinker Public Relations, an Award-winning, Full-service Strategic Communications Company

Dear Success Seeker . . .

Live each day as though it were your best! You have God-given talents unique to you and you alone. Take these skills and use them to the best of your abilities. Continue to grow them, improve them, and build upon them. With your gifts, pursue excellence with joy, humility, and gratefulness.

Respect authority, work hard (practice, practice, practice!), and be honest at all times. Never compromise the truth or your integrity. Be "other-focused," not "self-focused." Your life will be deeply enriched by serving others.

Create goals for yourself and be diligent in achieving those goals. Don't give up. In life, there are no shortcuts.

The Bible says, "A gentle answer turns away wrath, but a harsh word stirs up anger." Control your temper and what is uttered from your mouth. Words sting and cannot be retracted. Treat each person with a kind word and thoughtful gesture. That is critical in building relationships and succeeding in life. Treat all people with respect. Use discernment in making friends with individuals who are good influences, mentors, and role models. Flee those whose motives are destructive, mean-spirited, self-seeking, or evil.

Many times in life there will be difficult circumstances beyond your control. What you *can* control are your responses to those circumstances. Don't be discouraged, bitter, or angry. Remember, my friends, there are bumps and bruises in daily living. Choose joy. Your responses to your tough circumstances will dictate the quality of life you will lead. In life, pain is mandatory, but suffering is optional. It is a matter of choice.

More important, fear God. He has given you your capabilities, and He is worthy of your worship. God is good! Be sure to give Him credit for all your blessings.

Friends, go get 'em! Life is waiting to embrace you! God bless you!

In His service,
Cindy Brinker Simmons

Pastor Diane C. Smalley

Founding Member of the Council of Clergywomen of Metropolitan Detroit

Dear Success Seeker . . .

While I cannot tell your faith story, your "her-story," I certainly can tell mine. . . . The journey to the pulpit as pastor was a journey filled with tough spots, tight choices, hopeless days, and greedy nights. While pretending to be a solid student at the University of Arkansas at Fayetteville, I wasted time, energy, and money. After flunking out in Fayetteville, I spent too much time at the University of Arkansas at Pine Bluff trying to find myself by sitting in Smitty's (not the barbershop, the other Smitty's—the bar), spinning around on bar stools in the early afternoon, telling lies, trying to figure out the ins and outs of romance, making it through the day sober, and, Lord, through the nights, alive. After finally graduating, with honors, from Philander Smith College, I worked in places financed by foundations and federal grants that tackled social problems and fought poverty. I was overworked, underpaid, but on a mission. Individuals who were self-serving and greedy, and who robbed the innocent and devoured the poor, sometimes supervised my employment.

I received my call to the ministry in 1981, while engaged in the war on female poverty, while an active member of St. John Missionary Baptist Church in Little Rock, and while simultaneously attending Bible study sessions. The Sunday following public announcement of my call to preach before the Baptist body, and after noting the shocked and horrified response to the idea of a woman preaching, I became a member of the African Methodist Episcopal Church, acknowledged my call in that denomination, and was licensed to preach by the Twelfth Episcopal District of the African Methodist Episcopal Church in 1982.

Twenty years ago, at midnight, I took a rental truck to Georgia, heading to a seminary that still does not have the endowment presence of Princeton or Harvard. Within five years of receiving the license to preach, I was invited to join the Presbyterian Church (United States); received a ministry recognized by the Presbytery of Greater Atlanta as a valid ministry for ordination; and on my daughter's fourteenth birthday, I was ordained to the Ministry of Word and Sacrament in Sisters Chapel on the campus of Spelman College.

Opposition to female pastors remains a crude reality. The church represents one arena in which women leaders meet opposition; there remain other fields in which glass ceilings threaten to thwart professional aspirations. Remember that you can do all things and allow nothing negative to define your reality.

When words of reason no longer provide encouragement, have a melody in your heart. I listen to "I don't feel no ways tired, I've come too far from where I started from. Nobody told me that the road would be easy . . ."

Sincerely,
Diane C. Smalley

Bobbie R. Stevens, PhD

Founder and President of Unlimited Futures, LLC

Dear Success Seeker . . .

One of the most perplexing decisions of my life was choosing a career. There are so many choices possible. Many years ago when I was in college, I began to think about why some people are so much more successful than others.

I began to read the work of the renowned psychologist Abraham Maslow. When Maslow was in college he noticed that some people functioned from a more advanced level than the average person. He studied these people to understand how they differed from ordinary people. He discovered that these people were very healthy. They were also happy. He found that they were highly creative, highly accomplished, and highly intuitive. They had discovered a different way of knowing whatever they needed to know. Maslow coined the term *self-actualization* to describe this more advanced way of functioning. He said that ordinary people are motivated by needs, and are constantly looking for external ways to fulfill their needs and desires. On the other hand, self-actualized people had discovered their own *inner* ability to fulfill their needs and desires. Maslow said the self-actualized person is motivated by Being or motivated from within themselves. One difference seems to be inner versus outer focus.

When I found Maslow's works I realized that self-actualization had to be a human potential—one obviously well worth developing. There must be some way for all of us to become healthier, happier, more creative, and intuitive. I believed that my purpose was to discover a way for each of us to develop this advanced way of functioning within ourselves. Ten years later I discovered a process, which we can all use, to develop self-actualization within ourselves.

I was looking for something to help me quit smoking, when I found an article in a magazine about some breathing exercises that would help one quit. I contacted the teacher. She taught me the breathing exercises. She also taught me some stretching exercises. Then I found a book on meditation and focusing techniques. I put together a routine of these things that I started doing on a daily basis, and within a short period of time my whole life changed. I begin to feel younger, and more confident. My energy starting increasing, and my mind became very clear. I knew things that I had no way of knowing. While experimenting with this new way of functioning, I would ask questions, and the correct answers came to me. Then I asked to understand what role we each play in creating whatever we experience in our lives. I got a very clear vision of how we all create whatever we experience. I could see that there are principles of life that govern how we actually create our own experiences, and immediately knew that I could create whatever I wanted.

My advice to you is: don't settle for less than what is possible for you. The time has come for all of us to focus our attention on our own personal growth. Being more is the only way we will be able to give more. Please withdraw from all the stresses of your environment long enough to get to know the wonderful possibilities that are yours by discovering the power you have within yourself.

Bobbie R. Stevens

Susan L. Taylor

Editor Emerita of *Essence* Magazine; Founder of National Cares Mentoring Movement

Dear Success Seeker . . .

DO WHAT YOU LOVE!

Today I feel a zest for living, but there was a time when I felt stuck—when it seemed that nothing in my life was working. Money would come, then slip through my fingers. There was never enough. I felt poor because I was living poorly. In retrospect, I see that my own faulty thinking had come between me and my hopes and dreams. Although I didn't share it, inwardly I would tear myself down, would compare myself unfavorably with the many smart, skilled, and organized sisters in my world. And my impoverished thoughts and habits—dream killers—did their destructive work: they created circumstances and experiences that mirrored them.

It's how our intelligence works. What is impressed on our subconscious is magnified, multiplied, and made real in the world. We do create our own reality. So when fearful thoughts of deprivation or self-criticism come, we must slay them by contemplating and embodying the truth: My God shall supply all my needs according to His riches . . . I am made in the image and likeness of the Creator . . . The Lord is my shepherd, I shall not want. Remembering and repeating one spiritual truth overrides a thousand negative thoughts. And when we stir up our faith in the riches within us, all of life's blessings flow.

If we're not watchful, though, the demands of our daily lives consume us. Our hopes and dreams dim and diminish; we adjust and hardly notice. But our heart notices. The heart is where God lives in us. So when we follow our heart, our passion, we are led to infinite abundance. Move out of your head and into your heart, and your feelings and behavior change. You feel compassion—for yourself and for others. You know that each moment is a gift, a powerful and precious one, and that your passion is your divine assignment.

Do what you love, and prosperity will follow. And money is just part of it. The greater part is the clarity you'll feel about why you are here and where you are headed. Your life will have greater depth, breadth, and richness than ever before.

Do what you love. Maybe you're bored with your work. Discontent can be divine intervention, God's way of encouraging you to reexamine your path and use your unique talent. As you do more of what you love, you create abundance of the highest measure: peace, prosperity, joy. You become more passionate about the things that matter most to you.

Do what you love. Travel, teach, organize events. Write, paint, design Web sites, follow the financial markets. Do it for you, and, if you choose, do it for others and charge them for your efforts— turn your passion into your business.

Don't expect seamless transitions or instant success. Look honestly at your skills, and close any gap between them and your dreams. I did that work—and I'm still doing it. So I could better serve our people, I went to college for the first time in my midthirties. Now I want to deepen my spiritual studies; next is finance. Nothing new and great is created from the safety of our comfort zone.

As you make the stretch, know that you were born to win. The person you are destined to become is God's great idea.

Susan L. Taylor

Lillie Armstrong Thomas

**First Secretary to Dr. Martin Luther King Jr.;
Former Office Manager, Southern Christian
Leadership Conference**

Dear Success Seeker . . .

Once upon a time I was where you are in life—young and sometimes floundering. So as you read my letter to you it is my very sincere hope that you will receive, profit, prosper, and have GOOD
success in life from my words of WISDOM that are intended to
admonish and exhort and edify you.

There will be moments and situations in your precious life
when those about you—friends, associates, and even relatives—will
tell and coerce you to say yes when deep in your heart that still
small voice says NO. My prayer for you is that you will STOP, and
consider the long-range result of your actions even though it may
cause you to lose some friends and associates. Saying NO to things
that are not for our ultimate good usually comes at a high price
and sacrifice: this has been my personal experience. But success—

GOOD success—can be ours only when we are willing to make the sacrifice.

Remember! Jesus loves you, and I do too!

Love forever and always in Jesus,
Lillie Armstrong Thomas

Gae Veit

**Former Owner and CEO, Shingobee Builders, Inc.,
$50 Million Full-service Commercial
Construction Company; Enrolled Member
of Crow Creek Sioux Tribe**

Dear Success Seeker . . .

My discovered favorite role in life is that of grandmother, and I write to all women who come after me, not just as business mentor but to you personally—my granddaughters.

It is my sixtieth year on planet earth, and I am still in awe of life and all of its joys and struggles. But mostly in awe of God Himself! I am His child, uniquely created and chosen by Him, here to do the works He has purposed for me.

As founder and CEO of Shingobee Builders, Inc., a commercial general-contracting firm, I am seen as a role model for women stepping into nontraditional fields, a place where dreams and opportunities abound. I would encourage you to look beyond the norm for women, to places that pique your interest, then explore the possibilities.

Each granddaughter has been placed by God in a family where

she has inherited certain traits and gifts to make her dualfold walk and purpose unique. My father grew up on the Crow Creek Sioux reservation and enrolled me as a band member when I was born. My inheritance from father was a spirit of adventure and the gift of Native enrollment; from mother I received the gift of both faith and giving. All serve me in my pursuit and success in business and in the knowledge of who I am and God's purpose for me. Thus, peace!

And so, my granddaughters, I encourage you to know yourselves. Step outside yourself to see clearly by asking friends and family to write letters of who they see you to be and why God placed you in your chosen family. And I encourage you to know God. Your love affair with Him can only come by study of His Word, letters written to you by your Father and Creator. May you discover the peace of who you are and why you were created. Only then can you enjoy the journey into each facet of life: business, daughter, sister, wife, mother, and eventually that of grandmother.

Gae Veit

Brenda Wade, PhD

Award-winning and Renowned
Psychologist; Author

Dear Success Seeker . . .

It's been a long road to learn to care about myself, to make choices that allow me to feel loved and valued, and to rise to a level of success that allows me to help others to grow.

True transformation happens at the deepest inner level of consciousness, the spiritual. We are body, emotions, mind and spirit and we must exercise all parts of our being to continue to grow. Every morning focus on what you want to accomplish by writing it down and then praying, asking for guidance and help. Then sit quietly in meditation (you can focus on an image of light to steady your mind) and wait for the still small voice within to give you instructions. Most people don't hear an actual voice but rather get an impression, a feeling or an idea that just flashes up. Before you take any action—and yes, you must put all of this into action—ask yourself, "Will I learn to love myself more if I do commit this act?" Practice self-love in your thoughts, words, and especially actions. Did I mention actually taking time to care for yourself lovingly (get in that bubble bath!).

Embrace yourself with self-forgiveness, self-acceptance, and self-love.

Blessings of light and love,
Brenda Wade

Faye Wattleton

**President of the Center for the Advancement
of Women; First Black to Become President
of Planned Parenthood Federation
of America, Inc.**

Dear Success Seeker . . .

Be informed. Be vigilant! You can't defend your rights if you
don't understand them, if you don't know how you got them, and
if you don't know who wants to destroy them. Take nothing for
granted, for you will not take pains to protect your rights if you
don't understand that they can, and how they can, be taken away.

Do not shrink from power. Feel a sense of who you really are
deep within, and do not rely on the approval of others as your primary source of affirmation. You have the power within yourself to
create beneficial change for yourself and for others.

Don't ever compromise your fundamental rights. Would you
be willing to sit still if the government took control of the *New
York Times*? Wouldn't it be unthinkable to you if each edition were
reviewed by government censors? My daughter, the sanctity of
your body is even more precious.

Don't ever let anyone convince you that a cause cannot be won. It may take time and it may be painful, but nothing of value has ever been attained without struggle. So much is lost when we cannot summon the courage of our convictions.

Support other women. We must support each other when we speak out and when we challenge barriers. I deeply hope that the women of your generation will be more mutually supportive than the women of my time have learned to be.

You've been encouraged to be an independent thinker. In your brief life, encounters with injustice have energized your spirit of resistance. I've seen your reaction when you believed I was dealing with you unfairly; I've seen the sadness and indignation in your eyes when we sat together in the villages of the poorest women of the world. You've grown up in the thick of one of the most important social movements of the twentieth century. You've been taught the value of hard work and diligence. The doors of opportunity have been opened wide for you. But it's not the privilege to which we are born, but what we make of our lives that counts.

You must now continue the fight.

Faye Wattleton

Tene M. Wells

President of WomenVenture

Dear Success Seeker . . .

Every day I see women who are dissatisfied with their economic status or choice of employment. Many of these women didn't follow their passions to a life of rewarding work. They have forgone the careers they were trained to do because of discrimination or lack of encouragement, or in order to support their partners or raise their children. In many cases, their dreams were deferred for noble reasons.

As the president of WomenVenture, my mission is to help women achieve economic success and prosperity. We help women explore all their career options and gain the confidence to break barriers, make economically sound career choices, and follow their dreams. We help women attain the skills they need to get a job in a trade industry, like construction or cable installation, because they pay twice as much as fields that are predominated by women. We provide technical assistance and working capital for women who want to start their own business because self-employment offers the most flexibility for women trying to raise children and build a legacy. Our GirlVenture program encourages young girls to begin to plan their economic futures because it is never too early to start. We have helped over fifty-eight thousand women find economic and fulfilling work.

Unfortunately, even in this time of great advantages for many women, most women still think they will be supported the way women were over thirty years ago. Even with the opportunity to receive an education, the ability to own property, and the certainty that every woman has to take care of herself and her children, at some time in their lives, most women do not consider the impact of their youthful decisions on their economic future.

No matter what you want to be, there is something you can do as a young woman that is related to that dream—whether it's reading more about it, volunteering, interning, or even finding a mentor in your field of choice. And if you don't have a clue, you can work and find out why they love it. Above all, learn to see opportunity wherever you are. You'll be surprised at all the world has to offer you.

Your economic future is in your hands. Choose wisely and follow your dreams.

Sincerely,
Tene M. Wells

Shirley A. White, EdD

President of Success Images,
Career Coaching and Consulting Firm

Dear Success Seeker . . .

Many years ago, a good friend gave me some wonderful career advice. She said, "Listen to your heart. Knowing what you want is the first step toward getting it. That's where it all starts. And remember, to be truly successful, you need to be happy with what you're doing. Give your maximum effort to be the very best you are capable of becoming." These thoughts have greatly influenced me throughout my career, and I want to share them with you along with five steps that can enhance your ability to triumph over life's challenges.

Read the biographies of your heroes and other great books. They will inspire and give you insight. Set realistic and attainable goals. They will give you a much-needed sense of purpose and a vision that will keep you pressing on. Write down your goals. It helps to crystallize them. Set deadlines for accomplishing your goals, and remember the adage, "by the yard, it's hard; by the inch, it's a cinch." Be committed. Commitment gives you power. For no matter what comes your way, you never turn your eye from the goal. Commitment guarantees victory. If difficulties are thrust in front of you, you will go around, under, or through them. It's hard to keep committed people from success.

Be change oriented. Change helps you to refocus. Change gives you new opportunities. So rather than being too resistive, too reactive, and too closely tied to old habits, get out of your comfort zone. Stretch! View change as an exciting challenge, as the beginning of taking new and bold steps to achieving success. Think positively. I truly believe that attitude is the key to success or failure in most of life's endeavors. Everyone must deal with disappointment, setback, and temporary failure. When faced with a challenge, the attitude you choose determines your outcome. Choose to be positive.

Remember, success is a self-fulfilling prophecy. If you expect to succeed, you will! My best wishes are with you as you go forward to meet the challenges of life and achieve your highest aspirations.

Sincerely,
Shirley A. White

Frankie Berry Wise

Award-winning Professional Homemaker
and Cook; Animal Rights Activist

Dear Success Seeker . . .

As far back as I can remember; I have aspired to be an artist or a nurse—what a contrast in career goals. After arriving at Tuskegee Institute (University) in 1962, my love for art and nursing remained constant until I was married and started raising a family. Little did I know that my two lifelong pursuits would aid me so greatly in my child-rearing skills. My nursing and nurturing skills also made my task easier. I found that to be an effective "mother of five" and a "wife of one" required all of the craftiness and artistry that I could muster. In fact, I think I raised it to a new art form.

This leads me to the best advice I can provide you: talk less, listen more. In this capacity, you will have a closed mouth and open ears to take advantage of countless words of wisdom.

Undoubtedly, there is a time to talk. However, with appropriate and strategic listening and thinking, you can speak with both wisdom and knowledge. You will also logically know when, how, or if to talk.

And when you do speak, choose your words wisely and sensitively. Needless to say, words can follow you a lifetime. The power of words can make or break a nation, not to mention break or mend a heart!

Lastly, let me share with you a short note I wrote my oldest daughter during her transition from Ohio to Arkansas:

Dear Monica,

Loan only once to the same person, but try to never borrow. Offer as much help as you can, but not to be used. Invite only when you mean it, and visit unoften. Listen, but not gossip.

With love,
Mom

Good luck in all your future endeavors; and continue to read, work hard, listen and talk wisely, and strive for excellence!

Sincerely,
Frankie Berry Wise

Susan Ruth Witkowski

Entrepreneur of Life; Broker/Owner of
Sage Properties of Arkansas

Dear Success Seeker . . .

When I was a little girl I would ask my mother why I was born. There had to be some reason why I was put here on earth? Most of my adult life I have been searching for the answer to this question. I use to think I had this grand mission to accomplish. What I have learned is that life is a journey and part of our mission is simple: just be the best you can be each and every day. That means being a person of integrity, a tolerant person, a loving person, as well as living each day as though it were your last.

When I am in a tough spot or need to make an important decision I try to get quiet and ask God for guidance, and what would Jesus do if He were in my shoes. We are born such clean little spirits, and as we go through life other people impose their prejudices on us. Before long we are carrying baggage or into bondage to someone or something. One of the greatest gifts our journey holds is that we have the opportunity to remove each and every one of those Band-Aids.

The person who has purpose or sees some meaning to their life is going to survive. Take a step out into the world and live your journey! In the end, all that matters is that you are true to yourself. Comparing yourself to others means nothing. The earlier you learn how to paddle your own canoe, the further you will be down the stream of life, making a bigger impact on this world and for the future generations to come.

Life is the palette; you are the artist!

Carpe diem,
Susan Ruth Witkowski

Robin Wolaner

Former Executive Vice President, CNET
Media Group; Founder, *Parenting* Magazine

Dear Success Seeker . . .

When I was in college, I thought I needed to have a life plan. Looking back, at forty-seven, I realize that if I had made such a plan and stuck to it, I would have missed most of the great things that have happened in my life. So my first piece of advice on success is to allow for serendipity. You can surprise yourself: I never considered a career in business (my parents were an engineer and a teacher), nor did I fit any of the stereotypes for entrepreneurs. Since my founding of *Parenting* magazine has been a Harvard Business School case study for the past decade, and taught internationally as a model of entrepreneurial finance, I guess I became an entrepreneur despite myself.

When that case study is taught, women in business school always ask if I had had children when I founded the magazine. My answer—not politically correct for a feminist, as I am—is that I couldn't have done it if I'd had children at that time. So the second piece of advice is: you can do it all, just not all at once. Starting a company means working around the clock, every day. That just isn't consistent with pregnancy and infancy, as I learned years later when I had my two children.

Finally, my last piece of advice is to follow your interests and values; the money will take care of itself. Every job I ever took—particularly including the founding of *Parenting*—was a pay cut from my previous position, but a change I wanted to make to learn more or work with a different product or group of people. The only time I broke that rule, to take a promotion with Time Warner to run a bigger division than *Parenting*, was the only job I regret taking—the only career mistake I made.

Sincerely,
Robin Wolaner

Rose Wright

Proprietor of Mama Rose's Corner

Dear Success Seeker . . .

My name is Rose Marie Wright, and I was born in Little Rock, Arkansas, on February 24, 1938. I am the mother of five, grandmother of seven, and great-grandmother of eight. I am a living testimony that there is nothing, and I mean nothing, no matter how horrible the situation, where God is not right there. As success seekers, know that the Word says, "God will be with us. He will not fail us nor forsake us." Never forget it is not what we go through, but what keeps us.

Through the storm of life, remember the promises of God. Our God has promised us that nothing could separate us from the love of God (Romans 8:35–39). I have to say that in spite of all the trying times that I have encountered during my adult life, the Lord has truly blessed me. He has brought me through many tough times and shown me that He is my Savior. God alone is my provider and sustainer. Even though I don't always show it in my actions, without the Lord in my life, I am nothing.

I truly thank the Lord for allowing me to live for seventy years, and I hope for many more years. I still have a lot more growing to do in the Lord before my life is over. I want the Lord to be pleased with me. We all know that anyone desiring an intimate relationship with God has suffered. As the Word reads, "Do not withhold discipline from a child; if you punish him with the rod, he will not die. Punish him with the rod and save (his soul from death)."

By wisdom a house is built, and through understanding it is established. Through knowledge its rooms are filled with rare and beautiful treasures. I do believe that I can do all things through Christ who strengthens me. In all your success endeavors, may you seek ye first the kingdom of God, and His righteousness, and all these things (i.e., success) shall be added unto you. And as you pursue your success endeavors, may God get the glory; for He has done wonder things for me, yet they are for Him.

Sincerely,
Rose Wright

Rosalyn S. Yalow, MD

**American Medical Physicist; First American Woman
Trained in United States (Second Woman Ever)
to Win the Nobel Prize in Medicine**

Dear Success Seeker . . .

The success I have obtained in my life and career has come from
the knowledge acquired from people that encouraged me and excited
my interest in science. I believe anyone can learn from experiences
that will serve as positive inspirations to achieve goals and dreams.

We believe that each succeeding generation will be wiser than
its progenitors. We transmit to you, the next generation, the total
sum of our knowledge. Yours is the responsibility to use it, add to
it, and transmit it to your children.

We bequeath to you, the next generation, our knowledge but
also our problems. While we still live, let us join hands, hearts, and
minds to work together for their solution so that your world will be
better than ours and the world of your children even better.

Sincerely,
Rosalyn S. Yalow

Sandra Yancey

**Founder and CEO, eWomenNetwork, Inc.,
the Number One Resource for Promoting
and Connecting Women and
Their Businesses**

Dear Success Seeker . . .

One of the greatest secrets to your future success is to understand the power of your network. Make no mistake about it, everyone who makes it has a network.

It is no surprise to realize that much of what you learned today will quickly become obsolete. Technology and business are changing and evolving so rapidly. We simply cannot learn what we need to know fast enough to keep up with the whirl-wind of changes we face each and every day. Here's the good news: it's okay. You will find that the success of your future has more to do with knowing "who" versus knowing "how." That's right. Powerful people are no longer defined by their fancy titles, expensive clothes, or corner offices. Rather, powerful people are defined by their ability to make things happen and get things done, both for themselves and others.

Your network should be built on the foundation of some key constituents. The earlier you identify and build a solid relationship with them, the more stable and sustaining your network will be. Take inventory of your relationships now and be sure you can identify one mentor—someone who picks you and whose role is to provide you "access"; two role models—people you admire and wish to emulate; and three connectors—people who easily and willingly connect people to other people. Each one of these constituents will play a unique and important role in your continued growth and development.

To establish a growing and evolving relationship with your core constituents, you must first recognize, believe, and behave according to the philosophy of *"It takes teamwork to make the dream work."* It is through the spirit of abundance that you first demonstrate your own character and integrity of helping others. After all, how can you expect others to do for you what you are not first willing to do for them? The point here is, powerful networkers believe in "giving first." They constantly and consistently look for ways to share contacts, resources, information, and leads without the expectation of anything in return. They live the law of the universe: that is, you must give in order to receive. And, you inherently know that when you give freely and without expectations, you will be rewarded tenfold.

Savvy networkers show up! They put their face in the place; they are seen in the scene. They are attentive and alert wherever they go, whether it is a business function or the dry cleaner's. They always wear a smile (the only universal language) and generate conversation. They ask great questions and listen more than speak. They always try to leave a conversation with the gift of a lead handwritten on the back of their business card. They know that through helping others, they are helping themselves, and by helping themselves, they can repeat the cycle. In the end, success is not about ME; it's about WE. It really does take teamwork to make the dream work.

I wish you the best of luck in all you do. Just remember, "Give first, share always."

Sandra Yancey

Final Thought

WHO DO I ADMIRE MOST?

A s author of *Dear Success Seeker: Wisdom from Outstanding Women*, I have an immeasurable level of appreciation and admiration for each of you who were inspired to read this book and seek success. Therefore, I am strongly compelled to reflect back on one of my most treasured inspirations, *"Who Do I Admire Most?"*, written by Monica René Wise, my oldest sister, at age seventeen, as part of my contestant's speech for the 1983–84 "Miss Tuskegee Institute High School Pageant":

"Who Do I Admire Most?"

" . . . I admire,

- The woman who not only mothers her child, but the world as if it were her own;
- The man who loves his God, his country, and his neighbor as he loves himself;
- The teacher who wants her students to know all that she knows and more, and teaches unselfishly;
- The student who realizes he will always be a student, and has not only the obligation to learn but to teach;
- The person who befriends the friendless, who stands

strong when others seem to fall, who cares when no one else seems to care, who loves though he may not be loved;

· The individual who realizes that there is a chance of losing, but is a winner within herself.

There is no one who possesses a quality not to be admired. Who do I admire most? I admire you . . ."

Monica René Wise (© 1983)

Ironically, "success seeker" is applicable to each of these categories to alternatively read:

"Who Do I Admire Most?"

" . . . I admire,

· The success seeker who not only mothers her child, but the world as if it were her own;

· The success seeker who loves his God, his country, and his neighbor as he loves himself;

· The success seeker who wants her students to know all that she knows and more, and teaches unselfishly;

· The success seeker who realizes he will always be a student, and has not only the obligation to learn but to teach;

· The success seeker who befriends the friendless, who stands strong when others seem to fall, who cares when no one else seems to care, who loves though he may not be loved;

· The success seeker who realizes that there is a chance of losing, but is a winner within herself.

There is no success seeker who possesses a quality not to be admired. Who do I admire most? I admire you . . ."

As a final thought, I am confident that each uniquely crafted "Dear Success Seeker" letter will not only afford you an opportunity to embrace the qualities of success that you admire most, but also help you to create your own legacy of success to be admired and emulated for generations to come.

Successfully yours,
Michele Rhonda Wright

ABOUT THE AUTHOR

Michele R. Wright, PhD (formerly Michele R. Wise), a native of Tuskegee, Alabama, is a top-performing and multiple national and international award—winning corporate leader with a successful track record in education; electrical and industrial engineering; project, team, and total quality management; food, pharmaceutical, and biotechnology sales. She has worked with reputable Fortune 500 organizations including Genentech Biotech Company, Novartis Pharmaceuticals Corporation, Pfizer Pharmaceuticals, The Pillsbury Company, The Procter and Gamble Company, Honeywell, and Martin Marietta Corporation. She holds a BS degree in Electrical Engineering from Tuskegee University; a MS degree in Industrial Engineering/Engineering Management from the University of Tennessee Space Institute; and a PhD in Public Policy from the University of Arkansas at Fayetteville. Her extensive research of some of America's most outstanding women achievers (i.e., history makers, Nobel Prize winners, CEOs, university presidents, and leaders in business and the arts) served as inspiration for this book. She lives in North Little Rock, Arkansas, with her husband.